O9-BTJ-960

Robert L. Linn
University of Colorado at Boulder

Norman E. Gronlund
Professor Emeritus,
University of Illinois at Urbana-Champaign

Student Exercise Manual for

Measurement
and Assessment
in Teaching

Eighth Edition

Merrill,
an imprint of Prentice Hall
Upper Saddle River, New Jersey   *Columbus, Ohio*

Cover Photo: International Stock
Editor: Kevin M. Davis
Developmental Editor: Gianna Marsella
Production Editor: Julie Peters
Production Manager: Laura Messerly
Cover Designer: Dan Eckel

This book was printed and bound by Victor Graphics.

©2000 by Prentice-Hall, Inc.
Pearson Education
Upper Saddle River, New Jersey 07548

All rights reserved. No part of this book may be reproduced, in any form or by any means,
without permission in writing from the Publisher.

Printed in the United States of America

10 9 8 7 6 5 4

ISBN 0-13-878976-2

Prentice-Hall International (UK) Limited, *London*
Prentice-Hall of Australia Pty. Limited, *Sydney*
Prentice-Hall of Canada, Inc., *Toronto*
Prentice-Hall Hispanoamericana, S. A., *Mexico*
Prentice-Hall of India Private Limited, *New Delhi*
Prentice-Hall of Japan, Inc., *Tokyo*
Prentice-Hall (Singapore) Pte. Ltd., *Singapore*
Editora Prentice-Hall do Brasil, Ltda., *Rio de Janeiro*

TO THE STUDENT

There are 477 objective test items and more than 100 constructed-response items in this manual. Each set of items is based on a clearly stated learning goal, to illustrate how test items should be designed to measure specific types of student performance.

These exercises are intended to help you understand and apply the concepts and principles of educational measurement. Although they were especially prepared to use with the eighth edition of Measurement and Assessment in Teaching, efforts were made to emphasize the content and skills that are common to most beginning measurement courses.

The content and organization of this manual are as follows:

- The exercises are arranged by chapter and there are five pages of exercises for each chapter and for the statistics section in Appendix A.

- Each exercise page typically contains a series of selection-type items and supply-type problems, related to specific learning goals they are designed to measure.

- The 25 to 30 selection-type items for a given chapter enable students to check their knowledge and understanding of basic concepts. The answers on the back of each exercise provide immediate feedback.

- The supply-type problems for each chapter provide students with an opportunity to test their understanding further and to apply what they are learning to practical situations (e.g., constructing test items, developing performance-based assessment tasks and scoring guides, interpreting item analysis data, test scores, and other statistics). Where computation is involved, the final answer is provided on the back of the answer sheet.

Studying the textbook and doing the exercises in the manual should provide a sound foundation for using measurement and assessment in teaching.

CONTENTS

Chapter 6 - Planning Classroom Tests and Assessments

Chapter 7 - Constructing Objective Test Items: Simple Forms

Chapter 8 - Constructing Objective Test Items: Multiple-Choice Forms

Chapter 9 - Measuring Complex Achievement: The Interpretative Exercise

Chapter 10 - Measuring Complex Achievement: Essay Questions

Chapter 11 - Measuring Complex Achievement: Performance-Based Assessments

Chapter 12 - Portfolios

Chapter 13 - Assessment Procedures: Observational Techniques, Peer Appraisal, and Self-Report

Chapter 14 - Assembling, Administering, and Appraising Classroom Tests and Assessments

Chapter 15 - Marking and Reporting

Chapter 16 - Achievement Tests

Chapter 17 - Aptitude Tests

Chapter 18 - Test Selection, Administration, and Use

Chapter 19 - Interpreting Test Scores and Norms

Appendix A - Elementary Statistics

Exercise 1-A

HISTORY OF TEST-BASED REFORM

LEARNING GOAL: Identifies trends in the use of tests in educational reform efforts.

Directions: Indicate whether the following statements about the use of tests in reform efforts during the past forty years are **true (T)** or **false (F)** by circling the appropriate letter.

T   F   1.   Pressures for accountability have resulted in increased school testing.

T   F   2.   The rapid growth of minimum-competency testing requirements in the 1970s and early 1980s was stimulated by widely-held belief that high school graduates often lacked essential skills.

T   F   3.   There is public support for the use of test results to compare schools.

T   F   4.   The "Lake Wobegon Effect" clearly demonstrated that test-based comparisons of schools has improved education.

T   F   5.   Concerns that accountability leads to teaching to the test have contributed to calls for increased reliance on performance-based assessments.

T   F   6.   Content standards specify the minimum score required to pass a test.

LEARNING GOAL: Distinguishes between the purposes and characteristics of content standards and performance standards.

Directions: List the defining features of content standards and of performance standards. Distinguish between and describe the primary purposes of these two types of standards.

Content Standards:

Performance Standards:

(Why not have your instructor or a fellow student evaluate your items?)

Turn up bottom of page for answers
Copyright © 2000 by Merrill, an imprint of Prentice-Hall, Inc. All rights reserved.

Answers to Selection 1-A

1. T   2. T   3. T
4. F   5. T   6. F

Exercise 1-B

PERFORMANCE ASSESSMENTS

LEARNING GOAL: Identifies characteristics of and rationales for the use of performance assessments.

Directions: Indicate whether measurement specialists would **agree (A)** or **disagree (D)** with each of the following statements concerning performance assessments by circling the appropriate letter.

A   D   1.   The belief that testing and assessment shapes instruction has led to increased emphasis on performance assessments.

A   D   2.   Authentic assessment is routinely achieved by the introduction of performance assessments.

A   D   3.   Many proponents of performance assessments accept the idea that "what you test is what you get."

A   D   4.   Tasks requiring extended responses have been the target of most criticisms of testing and assessment.

A   D   5.   Anything that can be measured by a performance assessment task could also be measured by a multiple-choice test.

LEARNING GOAL: Identifies advantages and disadvantages of performance-based assessments.

Directions: List some of the major advantages and disadvantages of performance-based assessments.

Advantages:

Disadvantages:

(Why not have your instructor or a fellow student evaluate your items?)

Turn up bottom of page for answers
Copyright © 2000 by Merrill, an imprint of Prentice-Hall, Inc. All rights reserved.

Answers to Selection 1-B

1. A   2. D   3. A   4. D   5. D

Exercise 1-C
_____

NATIONAL AND INTERNATIONAL ASSESSMENT

LEARNING GOAL: Identifies characteristics and limitations of national and international assessments.

Directions: Indicate whether the following statements about national and international assessment are **true (T)** or **false (F)** for circling the appropriate letter.

T   F   1.   The National Assessment of Educational Progress (NAEP) enables schools to compare the performance of their students to the nation as a whole.

T   F   2.   NAEP provides a means of monitoring trends in the achievement of students 25 years.

T   F   3.   In addition to national results, NAEP now provides results for state-by-state comparisons on a voluntary basis.

T   F   4.   NAEP collects achievement data for students by both age and grade level.

T   F   5.   Comparisons of nations based on international assessments are as trustworthy as comparison of regions of the country based on NAEP results.

T   F   6.   Comparability of results in international assessments is assured by translating assessments to the languages spoken in different countries.

LEARNING GOAL: Identifies influences at the national level that may influence the role and nature of testing and assessment in the future.

Directions: Briefly describe actions of the federal government that are likely to influence testing and assessment in the future.

(Why not have your instructor or a fellow student evaluate your items?)

Copyright © 2000 by Merrill, an imprint of Prentice-Hall, Inc. All rights reserved.

Answers to Selection 1-C

1. F   2. T   3. T
4. T   5. F   6. F

Exercise 1-D

CURRENT TRENDS IN EDUCATIONAL MEASUREMENT

LEARNING GOAL: Identifies factors related to current trends in testing and assessment.

Directions: Indicate whether measurement specialists would **agree (A)** or **disagree (D)** with each of the following statements concerning current trends in testing and assessment by circling the appropriate letter.

A   D   1.   Computers are especially useful for adaptive testing.

A   D   2.   Computer-administered simulations of problems enable the measurement of complex skills not readily measured by paper-and-pencil tests.

A   D   3.   Despite concern about the quality of school programs, there has been a **demand** for **less** testing and assessment.

A   D   4.   Computerized adaptive tests increase efficiency by reducing the number of items that need to be administered to achieve reliable measurement for a given test taker.

A   D   5.   The focus on the consequences of testing and assessment has decreased in recent years.

A   D   6.   The computer provides the potential to present simulations that can measure the processes that student use to solve problems.

LEARNING GOAL: Describes advantages and limitations of expanded uses of computer-based tests and assessments.

Directions: Briefly describe some of the important advantages and major limitations of expanded uses of computer-based tests assessments.

Advantages:

Limitations:

(Why not have your instructor or a fellow student evaluate your items?)

Copyright © 2000 by Merrill, an imprint of Prentice-Hall, Inc. All rights reserved.

Answers to Selection 1-D

1. A   2. A   3. D
4. A   5. D   6. A

Exercise 1-E

_____

CONCERNS AND ISSUES IN TESTING AND ASSESSMENT

LEARNING GOAL: Identifies factors related to concerns and issues in testing and assessment.

Directions: Indicate whether test specialists would **agree (A)** or **disagree (D)** with each of the following statements describing concerns and issues in testing and assessment by circling the appropriate letter.

A   D   1.   Many of the criticisms of testing are the result of misinterpretation and misuse of test scores.

A   D   2.   A common misinterpretation of scores on tests and assessments is to assume they measure more than they do.

A   D   3.   Testing does **not** have any undesirable effects on students.

A   D   4.   If a particular group receives lower scores on a test, it means the test is biased against members of that group.

A   D   5.   It is good practice to post scores on standardized tests so that students in a class can see how their performance compares to that of their peers.

A   D   6.   Test anxiety may lower the performance of some students.

LEARNING GOAL: Lists the possible effects of students and parents examining school testing and assessment results.

Directions: List the advantages and disadvantages of the legal requirement that students and parents must be provided with access to school testing and assessment records.

Advantages:

Disadvantages:

(Why not have your instructor or a fellow student evaluate your items?)

Turn up bottom of page for answers
Copyright © 2000 by Merrill, an imprint of Prentice-Hall, Inc. All rights reserved.

Answers to Selection 1-E

1. A   2. A   3. D
4. D   5. D   6. A

Exercise 2-A

PRINCIPLES AND PROCEDURES OF CLASSROOM ASSESSMENT

LEARNING GOAL: Distinguishes between sound and unsound principles and procedures.

Directions: Indicate whether each of the following statements represents a **sound (S)** or **unsound (U)** principle or procedure of classroom assessment by circling the appropriate letter to the left of the statement.

S   U   1.   The first step in measuring classroom learning is to decide on the type of test to use.

S   U   2.   Classroom assessment should be based on objective data only.

S   U   3.   The type of classroom assessment used should be determined by the performance to be measured.

S   U   4.   Effective classroom assessment requires the use of a variety of assessment techniques.

S   U   5.   Assessment techniques should replace teacher observation and judgment.

S   U   6.   Error of measurement must always be considered during the interpretation of assessment results.

LEARNING GOAL: State the meaning of test, measurement, and assessment.

Directions: In your own words, state the meaning of each of the following terms.

Test:

Measurement:

Assessment:

(Why not have your instructor or a fellow student evaluate your items?)

Copyright © 2000 by Merrill, an imprint of Prentice-Hall, Inc. All rights reserved.

Answers to Selection 2-A

1. U 2. U 3. S
4. S 5. U 6. S

Exercise 2-B

CLASSROOM ASSESSMENT AND THE INSTRUCTIONAL PROCESS

LEARNING GOAL: Identifies how classroom assessment functions in the instructional process.

Directions: Indicate whether the textbook authors would **agree (A)** or **disagree (D)** with each of the following statements by circling the letter to the left of the statement.

A   D   1.   The main purpose of classroom assessment is to improve learning.

A   D   2.   The first step in both teaching and assessment is to determine the intended learning outcomes.

A   D   3.   Classroom assessments should not be given until the end of instruction.

A   D   4.   Instructional objectives should aid in selecting the types of assessment instruments to use.

A   D   5.   Assessment results should be used primarily for assigning grades.

A   D   6.   Classroom assessment always includes some form of testing.

LEARNING GOAL: Describes the role of instructional objectives.

Directions: Describe the role of instructional objectives in classroom assessment.

(Why not have your instructor or a fellow student evaluate your items?)

Copyright © 2000 by Merrill, an imprint of Prentice-Hall, Inc. All rights reserved.

Answers to Selection 2-B

1. A   2. A   3. D
4. A   5. D   6. D

Exercise 2-C
___

**MEANING OF PLACEMENT, FORMATIVE, DIAGNOSTIC,
AND SUMMATIVE ASSESSMENT**

LEARNING GOAL: Classifies examples of classroom assessment procedures.

Directions: For each of the following descriptions, indicate which **type of assessment** is represented by circling the appropriate letter using the following key.

KEY   P = Placement   F = Formative
         D = Diagnostic   S = Summative

P   F   D   S   1.   An achievement test is used to certify student mastery.

P   F   D   S   2.   Students are given a ten-item test to determine learning progress.

P   F   D   S   3.   A teacher observes the process used as a student solves arithmetic problems.

P   F   D   S   4.   Algebra students take an arithmetic test on the first day of class.

P   F   D   S   5.   Course grades are assigned.

P   F   D   S   6.   An assessment is given at the beginning of a new unit.

LEARNING GOAL: State examples of types of assessment procedures.

Directions: For each of the following types of assessment state one specific example that illustrates its use in some subject area.

Placement:

Formative:

Diagnostic:

Summative:

(Why not have your instructor or a fellow student evaluate your items?)

Turn up bottom of page for answers
Copyright © 2000 by Merrill, an imprint of Prentice-Hall, Inc. All rights reserved.

Answers to Selection 2-C

1. S   2. F   3. D
4. P   5. S   6. P

Exercise 2-D

MEANING OF CRITERION-REFERENCED AND NORM REFERENCED INTERPRETATIONS

LEARNING GOAL: Distinguishes between examples of each type of interpretation.

Directions: Indicate whether each of the following statements represents a **criterion-referenced (C)** interpretation or a **norm-referenced (N)** interpretation by circling the appropriate letter.

C   N   1.   Erik obtained the highest score on the reading test.

C   N   2.   Carlos can identify all of the parts of a sentence.

C   N   3.   Connie can type 60 words per minute.

C   N   4.   John earned an average score on an arithmetic test.

C   N   5.   Tonia defined only 20 percent of the science terms.

C   N   6.   Maria set up her laboratory equipment faster than anyone else.

LEARNING GOAL: Writes statements representing each type of interpretation.

Directions: Write three statements that represent **criterion-referenced** interpretations and three statements that represent **norm-referenced** interpretations.

Criterion-referenced interpretations:

Norm-reference interpretations:

(Why not have your instructor or a fellow student evaluate your items?)

Copyright © 2000 by Merrill, an imprint of Prentice-Hall, Inc. All rights reserved.

Answers to Selection 2-D

1. N 2. C 3. C
4. N 5. C 6. N

Exercise 2-E
_____

MEANING OF CONTRASTING TEST TYPES

LEARNING GOAL: Distinguishes between contrasting test types.

Directions: For each of the following test descriptions indicate which **test type** is represented by circling the letter to the left of each description using the following key.

KEY A = Informal   C = Mastery   E = Speed   G = Objective   I = Verbal
      B = Standardized   D = Survey   F = Power   H = Subjective   J = Performance

A   B   1.   A test using national norms for interpretation.

C   D   2.   A test used to measure many skills with just a few items for each skill.

E   F   3.   A test that all students are expected to complete.

G   H   4.   A test on which different scorers obtain the same results.

I   J   5.   A test requiring students to describe how to set up laboratory equipment.

LEARNING GOAL: Describes a test representing a given test type.

Directions: In the spaces below, write a brief description of a specific test representing each of the test types.

Survey test:

Mastery test:

Power test:

Objective test:

(Why not have your instructor or a fellow student evaluate your items?)

Copyright © 2000 by Merrill, an imprint of Prentice-Hall, Inc. All rights reserved.

Answers to Selection 2-E

1.B   2.D   3.F   4.G   5.I

Exercise 3-A

INSTRUCTIONAL OBJECTIVES AS LEARNING OUTCOMES

LEARNING GOAL: Distinguishes between statements of learning process and learning outcomes.

Directions: Indicate whether each of the following features describes a **learning process (P)** or a **learning outcome (O)**.

P   O   1.   Learns the meaning of terms.

P   O   2.   Develops a more favorable attitude toward reading.

P   O   3.   Demonstrates concern for the environment.

P   O   4.   Locates a position on a map.

P   O   5.   Practices interpreting charts and graphs.

P   O   6.   Describes the value of good study habits.

LEARNING GOAL: Writes well-stated outcomes.

Directions: In the spaces below (1) rewrite as learning **outcomes** each of the statements at the top of the page that were classified as learning **processes**, and (2) write three general statements of learning **outcomes** for a course of subject area.

1. Learning outcomes rewritten from process statements.

2. Three general learning outcomes for a course.

(Why not have your instructor or a fellow student evaluate your items?)

Turn up bottom of page for answers
Copyright © 2000 by Merrill, an imprint of Prentice-Hall, Inc. All rights reserved.

Answers to Selection 3-A

1. P 2. P 3. O
4. O 5. P 6. O

Exercise 3-B

DOMAINS OF THE TAXONOMY (COGNITIVE, AFFECTIVE, PSYCHOMOTOR)

LEARNING GOAL: Identifies examples of instructional objectives belonging to each **Taxonomy**.

Directions: Indicate the **Taxonomy** domain to which each of the following general instructional objectives belongs by circling the appropriate letter.

> KEY   A = Affective
>   C = Cognitive
>   P = Psychomotor

A   C   P   1.   Understands basic concepts.

A   C   P   2.   Appreciates the contributions of scientists.

A   C   P   3.   Evaluates a book.

A   C   P   4.   Operates a slide projector.

A   C   P   5.   Writes smoothly and legibly.

A   C   P   6.   Demonstrates an interest in science.

LEARNING GOAL: Writes general instructional objectives that fit each **Taxonomy** domain.

Directions: Write two general instructional objectives for each of the following domains of the **Taxonomy**.

Cognitive objectives:

Affective objectives:

Psychomotor objectives:

(Why not have your instructor or a fellow student evaluate your items?)

Turn up bottom of page for answers
Copyright © 2000 by Merrill, an imprint of Prentice-Hall, Inc. All rights reserved.

Answers to Selection 3-B

1. C 2. A 3. C
4. P 5. P 6. A

Exercise 3-C

SELECTING APPROPRIATE INSTRUCTIONAL OBJECTIVES

LEARNING GOAL: Distinguishes between sound and unsound criteria for selecting instructional objectives.

Directions: Indicate whether each of the following statements is a **sound (S)** or **unsound (U)** criterion for selecting instructional objectives, by circling the appropriate letter.

S   U   1.   Instructional objectives should be limited to those learning outcomes that can be measured objectively.

S   U   2.   Instructional objectives should be related to the goals of the school.

S   U   3.   Instructional objectives should be concerned primarily with knowledge of facts.

S   U   4.   Instructional objectives should be selected in terms of their feasibility.

S   U   5.   Instructional objectives should specify the intended learning outcomes.

LEARNING GOAL: Describes the importance of selecting appropriate instructional objectives.

Directions: In your own words, describe the importance of carefully selecting instructional objectives.

(Why not have your instructor or a fellow student evaluate your items?)

Turn up bottom of page for answers
Copyright © 2000 by Merrill, an imprint of Prentice-Hall, Inc. All rights reserved.

Answers to Selection 3-C

1. U 2. S 3. U 4. S 5. S

Exercise 3-D

STATING GENERAL INSTRUCTIONAL OBJECTIVES

LEARNING GOAL: Distinguishes between well-stated and poorly stated general instructional objectives.

Directions: For each of the following pairs of objectives, indicate the one that is **best stated** as a general instructional objective by circling the letter of your answer (A or B).

1. A   Reads supplementary references.
    B   Sees the importance of reading.

2. A   Is aware of the value of money.
    B   Comprehends oral directions.

3. A   Shows students how to make accurate computations.
    B   Judges the adequacy of an experiment.

4. A   Demonstrates proficiency in laboratory skills.
    B   Gains minimum proficiency in mathematics.

5. A   Studies weather maps.
    B   Constructs weather maps.

6. A   Is familiar with the use of the library.
    B   Locates references in the library.

LEARNING GOAL: Rewrites poorly stated objectives as **well-stated** general instructional objectives.

Directions: Rewrite as **well-stated** general instructional objectives each of the six poorly stated objectives at the top of the page.

1.

2.

3.

4.

5.

6.

(Why not have your instructor or a fellow student evaluate your items?)

Turn up bottom of page for answers
Copyright © 2000 by Merrill, an imprint of Prentice-Hall, Inc. All rights reserved.

Answers to Selection 3-D

1. A   2. B   3. B
4. A   5. B   6. B

Exercise 3-E

STATING SPECIFIC LEARNING OUTCOMES

LEARNING GOAL: Distinguishes between performance and non-performance statements of specific learning outcomes.

Directions: For each of the following pairs of specific learning outcomes, indicate the one that is stated in **performance terms**.

1.   A   States the principle.
       B   Realizes the value of the principle.

2.   A   Increases ability to read.
       B   Selects the main thought in a passage.

3.   A   Learns facts about current events.
       B   Relates facts in explaining current events.

4.   A   Distinguishes facts from opinions.
       B   Is aware that opinions should not be stated as facts.

5.   A   Grasps the meaning of terms when used in context.
       B   Defines the terms in his or her own words.

6.   A   Identifies the value of a given point on a graph.
       B   Determines the trend shown in a graph.

LEARNING GOAL: States specific learning outcomes in performance terms.

Directions: Write three specific learning outcomes, in **performance terms**, for each of the following general instructional objectives.

Knows basic terms.

Demonstrates good study habits.

Interprets a weather map.

(Why not have your instructor or a fellow student evaluate your items?)

Turn up bottom of page for answers

Copyright © 2000 by Merrill, an imprint of Prentice-Hall, Inc. All rights reserved.

Answers to Selection 3-E

1. A   2. B   3. B
4. A   5. B   6. A

Exercise 4-A

VALIDITY AND RELATED CONCEPTS

LEARNING GOAL: Identifies the nature of validity.

Directions: Indicate which of the following statements concerning validity are **correct (C)** and which are **incorrect (I)** by circling the appropriate letter.

C   I   1.   Validity refers to the test itself, not to the interpretations of test scores.

C   I   2.   Validity is a matter of degree (e.g., high, low).

C   I   3.   Validity is a general quality that applies to various uses of assessment results.

C   I   4.   Validity is a unitary concept.

C   I   5.   Validity refers to how consistently a test measures.

C   I   6.   Validity is adequately described by the correlation of assessment scores with a criterion measure.

LEARNING GOAL: Distinguishes among **validity, reliability**, and **usability**.

Directions: Briefly describe the key feature of each concept.

Validity:

Reliability:

Usability:

(Why not have your instructor or a fellow student evaluate your items?)

Turn up bottom of page for answers
Copyright © 2000 by Merrill, an imprint of Prentice-Hall, Inc. All rights reserved.

Answers to Selection 4-A

1. I   2. C   3. I
4. C   5. I   6. I

Exercise 4-B

MAJOR VALIDITY CONSIDERATIONS

LEARNING GOAL: Identifies characteristics of the major validity considerations.

Directions: for each of the following statements, indicate which **major validity consideration** is being described by circling the appropriate letter using the following key.

KEY   A = content
      B = construct
      C = test-criterion relationships
      D = consequences

A   B   C   D   1.   Can be expressed by an expectancy table.

A   B   C   D   2.   Is determined primarily by logical analysis.

A   B   C   D   3.   Evaluates what happens when assessment results are used.

A   B   C   D   4.   Typically requires more than one criterion.

A   B   C   D   5.   Emphasizes the representativeness of the sample of tasks.

A   B   C   D   6.   The results may be summarized by a single number.

LEARNING GOAL: Writes an example that illustrates each of the four major validity considerations.

Directions: Briefly describe an example of evidence that would be relevant for each major consideration.

Content

Construct

Test-Criterion Relationships:

Consequences:

(Why not have your instructor or a fellow student evaluate your items?)

Turn up bottom of page for answers
Copyright © 2000 by Merrill, an imprint of Prentice-Hall, Inc. All rights reserved.

Answers to Selection 4-B

1. C   2. A   3. D
4. B   5. A   6. C

Exercise 4-C

MEANING OF CORRELATION

LEARNING GOAL: Interprets correlation coefficients and the effects of various conditions on them.

Directions: In each of the following pairs of statements, select the statement that indicates the **greater degree of relationship** and circle the letter of your answer (A or B). Assume other things are equal.

1.   A   A correlation coefficient of .60.
         B   A correlation coefficient of .10.

2.   A   A predictive validity coefficient.
         B   A concurrent validity coefficient.

3.   A   A predictive validity coefficient of .70.
         B   A predictive validity coefficient of -.80.

4.   A   A correlation between test scores and a criterion measure obtained one week later.
         B   A correlation between test scores and a criterion measure obtained one year later.

5.   A   The predictive validity coefficient for a set of scores ranging from 20 to 100.
         B   The predictive validity coefficient for a set of scores ranging from 80 to 100.

LEARNING GOAL: Lists factors influencing a correlation coefficient.

Directions: List three factors that will cause correlation coefficients to be small.

(Why not have your instructor or a fellow student evaluate your items?)

Turn up bottom of page for answers
Copyright © 2000 by Merrill, an imprint of Prentice-Hall, Inc. All rights reserved.

Answers to Selection 4-C

1. A   2. B   3. B   4. A   5. A

Exercise 4-D

EXPECTANCY TABLE

LEARNING GOAL: Interprets an expectancy table.

Directions: In the expectancy table below, the row for each score level shows the **percentage** of students who earned a grade of A, B, C, D, or F. Review the table and answer the question following it ("Chances" means chances in 100).

Percentage of Students

Score	F	D	C	B	A	Total
115-134	0	12	20	26	42	100
95-114	10	18	18	24	30	100
75-94	32	26	18	18	6	100

_____ 1.   If Sara had a score of 120, what are her chances of obtaining a grade of A?

_____ 2.   If Bob had a score of 113, what are his chances of obtaining a failing grade.

_____ 3.   If Tanya had a score of 90, what are her chances of obtaining a grade of C or higher?

_____ 4.   How many times greater are Sara's chances than Tanya's of obtaining a grade of A?

_____ 5.   What score levels provides the **best** prediction?

_____ 6.   What score levels provides the **poorest** prediction?

LEARNING GOAL: Describes the advantages, limitations, and cautions in using expectancy tables.

Directions: In the appropriate spaces below, describe the advantages, limitations, and cautions in using expectancy tables.

Advantages:

Limitations:

Cautions in Interpreting:

(Why not have your instructor or a fellow student evaluate your items?)

Copyright © 2000 by Merrill, an imprint of Prentice-Hall, Inc. All rights reserved.

Answers to Selection 4-D

1. 42 2. 10   3. 42
4. 7   5. 115-134 6. 95-114

Exercise 4-E

FACTORS AND CONDITIONS INFLUENCING VALIDITY

LEARNING GOAL: Identifies the influence of assessment practices on validity.

Directions: Indicate what **influence** each of the following assessment practices is most likely to have on validity by circling the appropriate letter to the left of each statement, using the following key.

      KEY R = Raise validity; L = Lower validity.

R   L   1.   Increase item difficulty by using more complex sentence structure.

R   L   2.   Increase the number of items measuring each specific skill from five to ten.

R   L   3.   Replace multiple-choice items with short-answer items for measuring the ability to define terms.

R   L   4.   Replace multiple-choice items by laboratory performance tasks for measuring ability to conduct experiments.

R   L   5.   Use selection-type items instead of supply-type items to measure spelling ability.

R   L   6.   Use an essay test to measure factual knowledge of historical events.

LEARNING GOAL: Lists factors that lower assessment validity.

Directions: In the space provided below, list as many factors as you can think of that might lower the validity of a classroom assessment.

(Why not have your instructor or a fellow student evaluate your items?)

Turn up bottom of page for answers

Copyright © 2000 by Merrill, an imprint of Prentice-Hall, Inc. All rights reserved.

Answers to Selection 4-E

1. L 2. R 3. R
4. R 5. L 6. L

Exercise 5-A

COMPARISON OF VALIDITY AND RELIABILITY

LEARNING GOAL: Identifies similarities and differences between validity and reliability.

Directions: Indicate whether each of the following statements is characteristic of **validity (V)**, **reliability (R)**, or **both (B)**, by circling the appropriate letter to the left of the statement.

V   R   B   1.   Can be expressed by an expectancy table or regression equation.

V   R   B   2.   Refers to the consistency of a measurement.

V   R   B   3.   Is often based on a comparison with an external criterion.

V   R   B   4.   Refers to the results of a test rather than the test itself.

V   R   B   5.   Compares performance on two halves of an assessment.

V   R   B   6.   Contributes to more effective classroom teaching.

LEARNING GOAL: Explains the relationship between validity and reliability.

Directions: In the appropriate spaces below, briefly explain each of the following statements.

1. If assessment results are highly valid, they will also be highly reliable.

2. If assessment results are highly reliable, they may or may not be valid.

3. In selecting an assessment, validity has priority over reliability.

(Why not have your instructor or a fellow student evaluate your items?)

Copyright © 2000 by Merrill, an imprint of Prentice-Hall, Inc. All rights reserved.

Answers to Selection 5-A

1. V 2. R 3. V
4. B 5. R 6. B

Exercise 5-B

_____

METHODS FOR DETERMINING RELIABILITY

LEARNING GOAL: Distinguishes among the methods for determining reliability.

Directions: For each of the following statements, indicate **which method** of determining reliability is being described by circling the appropriate letter using the following key.

KEY: A = Test-retest, same form; B = Equivalent form, immediate;
        C = Equivalent form, time interval; D = Split-half.

A   B   C   D   1.   Provides an inflated reliability coefficient for a speeded test.

A   B   C   D   2.   Usually provides the smallest reliability for a given assessment.

A   B   C   D   3.   Is best for determining the stability of assessment results.

A   B   C   D   4.   Does not indicate consistency of performance over different samples of items.

A   B   C   D   5.   Correlation coefficient must be adjusted with the Spearman-Brown formula.

A   B   C   D   6.   Best indicator of the adequacy of the test sample.

LEARNING GOAL: Summarizes the procedure for obtaining various types of reliability coefficients.

Directions: Briefly describe the **procedure for obtaining** each type of reliability coefficient.

Test-retest:

Equivalent forms:

Split-half:

Inter-rater agreement:

(Why not have your instructor or a fellow student evaluate your items?)

Copyright © 2000 by Merrill, an imprint of Prentice-Hall, Inc. All rights reserved.

Answers to Selection 5-B

1. D   2. C   3. A
4. A   5. D   6. B

Exercise 5-C

RELATING RELIABILITY TO THE USE OF ASSESSMENT RESULTS

LEARNING GOAL: Selects the reliability method that is most relevant to a particular use of assessment results.

Directions: For each of the following objectives, select the reliability method that is **most relevant** by circling the appropriate letter using the following key.

> KEY: T = Test-retest (time interval), E = Equivalent form (immediate), S = Split-half,
> I = inter-rater consistency.

T   E   S   I   1.   Determining whether test scores on school records are still dependable.

T   E   S   I   2.   Selecting an achievement test to measure growth over one school year.

T   E   S   I   3.   Selecting a highly speeded test.

T   E   S   I   4.   Evaluating the adequacy of judgmental scoring of performances on a complex task.

T   E   S   I   5.   Seeking support for the adequacy of the sample of test items.

T   E   S   I   6.   Determining whether an informal classroom assessment has internal consistency.

LEARNING GOAL: Justifies the selection of a reliability method for a particular test use.

Directions: For each of statements 1-6 above, write a sentence or two to **justify** why you think the selected reliability method would provide the most relevant information for that particular use.

1.

2.

3.

4.

5.

6.

(Why not have your instructor or a fellow student evaluate your items?)

Copyright © 2000 by Merrill, an imprint of Prentice-Hall, Inc. All rights reserved.

Answers to Selection 5-C

1. T   2. E   3. E
4. I   5. E   6. S

Exercise 5-D

RELIABILITY COEFFICIENT AND STANDARD ERROR OF MEASUREMENT

LEARNING GOAL: Identifies the similarities and differences between the two basic methods of expressing reliability.

Directions: Indicate whether each of the following statements is more characteristic of the **reliability coefficient (R)**, the **standard error of measurement (E)**, or **both (B)** by circling the appropriate letter to the left of the statement.

R   E   B   1.   Indicates the degree to which a set of scores contains error.

R   E   B   2.   Remains relatively constant from one group to another.

R   E   B   3.   Cannot be computed without the other.

R   E   B   4.   Useful in selecting a test for a particular grade.

R   E   B   5.   Increases as the spread of scores increases.

R   E   B   6.   Would be zero if the test were perfectly reliable.

LEARNING GOAL: Describes the use of standard error in interpreting test scores.

Directions: In the appropriate spaces below describe how confidence bands (error bands) are used to interpret each of the following.

1. An individual test score.

2. The difference between two test scores.

(Why not have your instructor or a fellow student evaluate your items?)

Copyright © 2000 by Merrill, an imprint of Prentice-Hall, Inc. All rights reserved.

Answers to Selection 5-D

1. B   2. E   3. E
4. B   5. R   6. E

Exercise 5-E

FACTORS INFLUENCING RELIABILITY AND INTER-RATER CONSISTENCY

LEARNING GOAL: Identifies the influence of assessment practices on reliability.

Directions: Indicates whether each of the following practices is most likely to **raise (R)**, **lower (L)**, or have **no effect (N)** on reliability.

R   L   N   1.   Add more items like those in the test.

R   L   N   2.   Remove ambiguous tasks from the assessment.

R   L   N   3.   Add five items that everyone answers correctly.

R   L   N   4.   Replace a multiple-choice test with an essay test.

R   L   N   5.   Modify the assessment tasks to obtain a wide spread of scores.

R   L   N   6.   Replace a 10-item multiple-choice quiz with a 10 item true-false quiz.

LEARNING GOAL: Computes and interprets inter-rater consistency expressed as the percent of exact agreement.

Directions: Using the information from the following table compute the percent exact agreement for the scores provided by two independent raters.

		Scores assigned by Rater 2				
	Score	1	2	3	4	Row Total
Scores	4	1	1	4	12	17
Assigned	3	1	5	17	6	29
by	2	6	18	7	1	32
Rater 2	1	16	5	1	0	22
	Column Total	23	29	29	19	100

Percent exact agreement =

Briefly interpret the results.

(Why not have your instructor or a fellow student evaluate your items?)

Copyright © 2000 by Merrill, an imprint of Prentice-Hall, Inc. All rights reserved.

Answers to Selection 5-E

1. R   2. R   3. N
4. L   5. R   6. L   63%

Exercise 6-A

TYPES AND USES OF CLASSROOM TESTS AND ASSESSMENTS

LEARNING GOAL: Relates type of test item or assessment task to information needed.

Directions: For each of the following questions, indicate which type of test item or assessment task would provide the **most useful information** by circling the appropriate letter to the left of the question.

KEY   P = Placement
       F = Formative
       S = Summative

P   F   S   1.   Are students making satisfactory progress in learning to make connections among major mathematical concepts?

P   F   S   2.   What types of errors are student making in learning grammar?

P   F   S   3.   Should Carman be encouraged to enroll in an advanced mathematics course?

P   F   S   4.   Is Michael ready for instruction on the new unit?

P   F   S   5.   What final grade should Lizanne receive in the science course?

P   F   S   6.   How do my students rank in achievement.

LEARNING GOAL: States whether a criterion-referenced or norm-referenced test is more useful for a particular use and justifies the choice.

Directions: For each of the questions 1-6 above, (1) state whether a **criterion-referenced test** or a **norm-referenced test** would provide the more useful information, and (2) explain, in a sentence or two, why you think that test type would be more useful.

1.

2.

3.

4.

5.

6.

(Why not have your instructor or a fellow student evaluate your items?)

Copyright © 2000 by Merrill, an imprint of Prentice-Hall, Inc. All rights reserved.

Answers to Selection 6-A

1. F   2. F   3. P
4. P   5. S   6. S

Exercise 6-B

SPECIFICATIONS FOR CLASSROOM TESTS AND ASSESSMENTS

LEARNING GOAL: Identifies the procedures involved in preparing specifications for classroom tests and assessments.

Directions: For each of the following statements, indicate whether the procedure is a **desirable (D)** or **undesirable (U)** practice when preparing specifications for test and assessments, by circling the appropriate letter to the left of the statement.

D   U   1.   Start by identifying the intended learning outcomes.

D   U   2.   Limit the specifications to those outcomes that can be measured objectively.

D   U   3.   Consider the instructional emphasis when specifying the sample of items and tasks.

D   U   4.   Increase the relative weighting of topics by including more items on those topics.

D   U   5.   Use a table of specifications for summative tests only.

D   U   6.   Consider the purpose of testing when determining item difficulty.

LEARNING GOAL: Explains the importance and nature of using a table of specifications.

Directions: Briefly explain each of the following statements in the space that follows it.

1.   Well-defined specifications contribute to validity.

2.   Well-defined specifications contribute to interpretability of the results.

3.   Tables of specifications may differ for end of unit and end of course assessments.

(Why not have your instructor or a fellow student evaluate your items?)

Copyright © 2000 by Merrill, an imprint of Prentice-Hall, Inc. All rights reserved.

Answers to Selection 6-B

1. D 2. U 3. D
4. D 5. U 6. D

Exercise 6-C

USE OF OBJECTIVE ITEMS AND PERFORMANCE ASSESSMENT TASKS

LEARNING GOAL: Identifies whether objective items or performance assessment tasks are more appropriate for a given condition.

Directions: For each of the following conditions, indicate whether **objective (O)** items or **performance (P)** assessment tasks would be more appropriate, by circling the correct letter to the left of each statement.

O   P   1.   A broad sampling of learning outcomes is desired.

O   P   2.   The need is to measure ability to organize.

O   P   3.   Time available to prepare test or assessment is short.

O   P   4.   Time available for scoring is short.

O   P   5.   The need is for measuring knowledge of important facts and major concepts covered throughout the semester.

O   P   6.   The need is to measure learning at the synthesis level.

LEARNING GOAL: States whether objective items or performance tasks are more useful for measuring a particular instructional objective and justifies the choice.

Directions: For each of the following general instructional objectives, (1) state whether **objective** items or **performance** tasks would be more appropriate, and (2) explain, in a sentence or two, why you think that approach would be more appropriate.

1.   Knows specific facts.

2.   Interprets a weather map.

3.   Evaluates a plan for an experiment.

(Why not have your instructor or a fellow student evaluate your items?)

Copyright © 2000 by Merrill, an imprint of Prentice-Hall, Inc. All rights reserved.

Answers to Selection 6-C

1. O 2. P 3. P
4. O 5. O 6. P

Exercise 6-D

SELECTING SPECIFIC OBJECTIVE-TYPE ITEMS FOR CLASSROOM TESTS

LEARNING GOAL: Identifies the most relevant objective-type items for a given specific learning outcome.

Directions: Indicate the type of objective test item that is most appropriate for measuring each of the specific learning outcomes listed below by circling the appropriate letter to the left of the outcome, using the following key.

KEY A = Short answer, B = True-false, C = Matching, D = Multiple-choice.

A B C D 1. Relates inventors and their inventions.

A B C D 2. Distinguishes between correct and incorrect statements.

A B C D 3. Recalls chemical formulas.

A B C D 4. Identifies the correct date for a historical event.

A B C D 5. Reduces fractions to lowest terms.

A B C D 6. Selects the best reason for an action.

LEARNING GOAL: States specific learning outcomes that can be measured most effectively by each item type.

Directions: For each of the following types of objective test items, state two **specific learning outcomes** that can be most effectively measured by that item type.

Short-answer:

True-false:

Matching:

Multiple-choice:

(Why not have your instructor or a fellow student evaluate your items?)

Turn up bottom of page for answers
Copyright © 2000 by Merrill, an imprint of Prentice-Hall, Inc. All rights reserved.

Answers to Selection 6-D

1. C   2. B   3. A
4. D   5. A   6. D

Exercise 6-E

PREPARING CLASSROOM TESTS AND ASSESSMENTS

LEARNING GOAL: Distinguishes between sound and unsound procedures for construction classroom tests and assessments.

Directions: Indicate whether each of the procedures listed below is **sound (S)** or **unsound (U)** in the construction of classroom tests and assessments by circling the appropriate letter to the left of the statement.

S   U   1.   Using a table of specification in test preparation.

S   U   2.   Writing more test items and assessment tasks than needed.

S   U   3.   Including a large number of items and tasks for each interpretation.

S   U   4.   Writing items on the day before testing.

S   U   5.   Including some clues on items to aid slow learners.

S   U   6.   Putting items and tasks aside for awhile before reviewing them.

LEARNING GOAL: Describes the role of item difficulty in preparing classroom tests.

Directions: Describe what is appropriate item difficulty for tests that are designed for each particular type of interpretation and explain why they differ.

Norm-referenced interpretation:

Criterion-referenced interpretation:

Why they differ:

(Why not have your instructor or a fellow student evaluate your items?)

Turn up bottom of page for answers
Copyright © 2000 by Merrill, an imprint of Prentice-Hall, Inc. All rights reserved.

Answers to Selection 6-E

1. S   2. S   3. S
4. U   5. U   6. S

Exercise 7-A

CHARACTERISTICS OF SHORT-ANSWER, TRUE-FALSE, AND MATCHING ITEMS

LEARNING GOAL: Distinguishes among the characteristics of different item types.

Directions: Indicate which type of objective test item best fits each of the characteristics listed below by circling the appropriate letter, using the following key.
KEY: S = Short answer, T = True-false, M = Matching.

S   T   M   1.   Is classified as a supply-type item.

S   T   M   2.   Most effective where classification is involved.

S   T   M   3.   Is most influenced by guessing.

S   T   M   4.   Is most difficult to score.

S   T   M   5.   Directions are most difficult to write for this type.

S   T   M   6.   Correct answer may be obtained on the basis of misinformation.

LEARNING GOAL: States advantages and limitations of each item type.

Directions: For each of the following types of objective test items, state one advantage and one limitation.

Short-answer item
     Advantage:

     Limitation:

True-false item
     Advantage:

     Limitation:

Matching items
     Advantage:

     Limitation:

(Why not have your instructor or a fellow student evaluate your items?)

Copyright © 2000 by Merrill, an imprint of Prentice-Hall, Inc. All rights reserved.

Answers to Selection 7-A

1. S   2. M   3. T
4. S   5. M   6. T

Exercise 7-B

EVALUATING AND IMPROVING SHORT-ANSWER ITEMS

LEARNING GOAL: Identifies common faults in short-answer items.

Directions: Indicate the **type of fault**, if any, in each of the following short-answer items by circling the appropriate letter, using the following key.

> KEY   A = has no faults, B = Has more than one correct answer,
>   C = Contains clue to the answer

A   B   C   1.   John Glenn first orbited the earth in _____.

A   B   C   2.   In what year did Borgoyne surrender to Saratoga? _____.

A   B   C   3.   The United Nations Building is located in the city of _____ _____.

A   B   C   4.   An animal that eats only plants is classified as _____.

A   B   C   5.   Test specifications can be indicated by a table of _____.

A   B   C   6.   Abraham Lincoln was born in _____.

LEARNING GOAL: Improves defective short-answer items.

Directions: Rewrite as **well-constructed** short-answer items each of the faulty items in 1 - 6 above. If an item has not faults, write **no faults** in the space.

1.

2.

3.

4.

5.

6.

(Why not have your instructor or a fellow student evaluate your items?)

Turn up bottom of page for answers
Copyright © 2000 by Merrill, an imprint of Prentice-Hall, Inc. All rights reserved.

Answers to Selection 7-B

1. B 2. A 3. C
4. A 5. C 6. B

Exercise 7-C

EVALUATING AND IMPROVING TRUE-FALSE ITEMS

LEARNING GOAL: Identifies common faults in true-false items.

Directions: Indicate the **type of fault**, if any, in each of the following true-false items by circling the appropriate letter, using the following key.

      KEY   A = Has no faults, B = is ambiguous, C = Contains a clue to the answer,
                 D = Opinion state (**not** true or false).

A   B   C   D   1.   Camping is fun for the entire family.

A   B   C   D   2.   A parasite may provide a useful function.

A   B   C   D   3.   The best place to study is in a quiet room.

A   B   C   D   4.   A nickel is larger than a dime.

A   B   C   D   5.   Abraham Lincoln was born in Kentucky.

A   B   C   D   6.   True-false statements should never include the word always.

LEARNING GOAL: Improves defective true-false items.

Directions: Rewrite as **well-constructed** true-false items each of the faulty items in 1-6 above. If an item has not faults, write **no faults** in the space.

1.

2.

3.

4.

5.

6.

(Why not have your instructor or a fellow student evaluate your items?)

Turn up bottom of page for answers
Copyright © 2000 by Merrill, an imprint of Prentice-Hall, Inc. All rights reserved.

Answers to Selection 7-C

1. D   2. C   3. D
4. B   5. A   6. C

Exercise 7-D

EVALUATING AND IMPROVING MATCHING ITEMS

LEARNING GOAL: Identifies common faults in a matching exercise.

Directions: Indicate the specific faults in the following matching exercise by circling the appropriate letter below the exercise   (Y = yes, N = no).

Directions: Match the items in the two columns.

Column I	Column II
____1. Wind vane	A. Used to measure temperature
____2. Tornado	B. Water vapor in the air
____3. Humidity	C. Violent storm
____4. Thermometer	D. Used to measure wind direction

Y   N   1.   Directions are inadequate.

Y   N   2.   Columns are inappropriately placed.

Y   N   3.   Clues are provided in the answers.

Y   N   4.   List of responses is too short.

Y   N   5.   Order of responses is improper.

Y   N   6.   Matching exercise lacks homogeneity.

LEARNING GOAL: Improves a defective matching exercise.

Directions: In the space below, rewrite the matching exercise at the top of the page. You may (1) add material, (2) delete material, or (3) rework it into more than one exercise, and or course should cover the same type of material.

(Why not have your instructor or a fellow student evaluate your items?)

Copyright © 2000 by Merrill, an imprint of Prentice-Hall, Inc. All rights reserved.

Answers to Selection 7-D

1. Y 2. Y 3. Y
4. Y 5. Y 6. Y

Exercise 7-E

CONSTRUCTING SHORT-ANSWER, TRUE-FALSE, AND MATCHING ITEMS

LEARNING GOAL: Constructs sample test items that are relevant to stated learning outcomes.

Directions: In the spaces provided, construct (1) two short-answer items (one in question form and one in incomplete statement form), (2) four true-false items, and (3) one four-item matching exercise. State the specific learning outcome for each item or set of items.

Short-answer item (question form)

Outcome:

Item:

Short-answer item (incomplete statement form)

Outcome:

Item:

True-false items

Outcome:

Items:

     1.

     2.

     3.

     4.

Matching exercise

Outcome:

Directions:

Column I	Column II
____1.	
____2.	
____3.	
____4.	
____5.	

Why not have your instructor or a fellow student evaluate your items?)

Copyright © 2000 by Merrill, an imprint of Prentice-Hall, Inc. All rights reserved.

Exercise 8-A

CHARACTERISTICS OF MULTIPLE-CHOICE ITEMS

LEARNING GOAL: Identifies the advantages and limitations of multiple-choice items in comparison to other item types.

Directions: The following statements compare multiple-choice (MC) items to other item types with regard to some specific characteristic or use. Indicate whether **test specialists** would **agree (A)** or **disagree (D)** with each statement by circling the appropriate letter.

A   D   1.   MC items avoid the possible ambiguity of the short-answer item.

A   D   2.   MC items are easier to construct than true-false items.

A   D   3.   MC items have less need for homogeneous material than the matching exercise

A   D   4.   MC items can be more reliably scored than short-answer items.

A   D   5.   MC items can measure **all** learning outcomes effectively.

A   D   6.   MC items have higher reliability per item than true-false items.

LEARNING GOAL: Lists the characteristics of an effective multiple-choice item.

Directions: List the important characteristics of each of the following parts of a multiple-choice item.

Item Stem:

Correct Answer:

Distracters:

(Why not have your instructor or a fellow student evaluate your items?)

Turn up bottom of page for answers
Copyright © 2000 by Merrill, an imprint of Prentice-Hall, Inc. All rights reserved.

Answers to Selection 8-A

1. A 2. D 3. A
4. A 5. D 6. A

Exercise 8-B

EVALUATING STEMS OF MULTIPLE-CHOICE ITEMS

LEARNING GOAL: Distinguishes between effective and ineffective stems for multiple-choice items.

Directions: For each of the following pairs, indicate which element would make the most effective stem for a multiple-choice item by circling its letter (A or B).

1. A   Why did the cost of energy rise so rapidly in the 1970s?
    B   Which one of the following statements is true about energy?

2. A   Achievement tests should
    B   Achievement tests are useful for

3. A   A whale is a
    B   Whales are classified as

4. A   Aluminum, which is finding many new uses, is made from
    B   Aluminum is made from

5. A   The man who first explored Lake Michigan was
    B   The Frenchman who first explored Lake Michigan was

6. A   Which of the following illustrates what is meant by climate?
    B   Which of the following does not illustrate what is meant by climate?

LEARNING GOAL: Describes the faults in ineffective stems for multiple-choice items.

Directions: For each of the ineffective stems in 1-6 above, **briefly describe the type of fault** it contains.

1.

2.

3.

4.

5.

6.

(Why not have your instructor or a fellow student evaluate your items?)

Turn up bottom of page for answers
Copyright © 2000 by Merrill, an imprint of Prentice-Hall, Inc. All rights reserved.

Answers to Selection 8-B

1. A   2. B   3. B
4. B   5. B   6. A

Exercise 8-C

EVALUATING ALTERNATIVES USED IN MULTIPLE-CHOICE ITEMS

LEARNING GOAL: Distinguishes between effective and ineffective use of alternatives in multiple-choice items.

Directions: For each of the following multiple-choice item stems, there are two sets of alternatives. Indicate which set would make the most effective alternatives for the items by circling the letter (A or B). The items are kept simple and the alternatives are place across the page to save space.

1.   A United State astronaut first stepped on the moon in
    A   (1) 1967   (2) 1968   (3) 1969   (4) 1970
    B   (1) 1959   (2) 1969   (3) 1979   (4) 1989

2.   Who was the 33rd President of the United States
    A   (1) Lincoln   (2) Wilson   (3) Harding   (4) Truman
    B   (1) Roosevelt   (2) Truman   (3) Eisenhower (4) Kennedy

3.   Which of the following represents what is meant by reforestation?
    A   (1) Cutting   (2) Replanting (3) Spraying   (4) Surveying
    B   (1) Recutting   (2) Replanting (3) Spraying   (4) Resurveying

4.   Which of the following best describes observable student performance?
    A   (1) Constructs   (2) Fears   (3) Realizes   (4) Thinks
    B   (1) Constructs   (2) Fears   (3) Realizes   (4) None of these

LEARNING GOAL: Describes the faults in ineffective sets of alternatives.

Directions: For each of the ineffective sets of alternatives in 1-4 above, briefly describe the type of fault it contains.

1.

2.

3.

4.

(Why not have your instructor or a fellow student evaluate your items?)

Copyright © 2000 by Merrill, an imprint of Prentice-Hall, Inc. All rights reserved.

Answers to Selection 8-C

1. A   2. B   3. B   4. B

Exercise 8-D

EVALUATING AND IMPROVING MULTIPLE-CHOICE ITEMS

LEARNING GOAL: Identifies common faults in multiple-choice items.

Directions: Indicate the major type of fault, if any, in each of the following multiple-choice items by circling the appropriate letter, using the following key. The alternatives are placed across the pages to save space.

     KEY A = No fault, B = Stem is inadequate, C = Contains inappropriate distracters,
          D = Contains a clue to the answer

A   B   C   D   1.   Reliability (a) means consistency (b) is the same as objectivity
                        (c) refers to usability (d) is a synonym for interpretability.

A   B   C   D   2.   The characteristic that is most desired in test results is (a) consistency
                        (b) reliability (c) stability (d) validity

A   B   C   D   3.   If a test is lengthened, its reliability will (a) decrease (b) increase
                        (c) stay the same (d) none of these

A   B   C   D   4.   A method of determining reliability that requires correlating scores
                        from two halves of a test is called (a) equivalent forms (b) Kuder-
                        Richardson method (c) split-half method (d) test-retest method

LEARNING GOAL: Improves defective multiple-choice items.

Directions: Rewrite as **well-constructed** multiple-choice items each of the faulty items in 1-4 above. If an item has no faults, write **no faults** in the space.

1.

2.

3.

4.

(Why not have your instructor or a fellow student evaluate your items?)

Turn up bottom of page for answers
Copyright © 2000 by Merrill, an imprint of Prentice-Hall, Inc. All rights reserved.

Answers to Selection 8-D

1.B 2.C 3.C 4.D

CONSTRUCTING MULTIPLE-CHOICE ITEMS

LEARNING GOAL: Constructs sample multiple-choice items that are relevant to stated learning outcomes.

Directions: In some subject area you have studied or plan to teach, construct one multiple-choice item for each of the general instructional objectives listed below.

Knows basic terms:

      Outcome:

      Item:

Knows specific facts

      Outcome:

      Item:

Understands principles (or facts)

      Outcome:

      Item:

Applies principles or facts

      Outcome:

      Item:

(Why not have your instructor or a fellow student evaluate your items?)

Copyright © 2000 by Merrill, an imprint of Prentice-Hall, Inc. All rights reserved.

Exercise 9-A

CHARACTERISTICS OF INTERPRETIVE EXERCISES

LEARNING GOAL: Identifies the advantages and limitations of interpretive exercises in comparison to other item types.

Directions: The following statements compare the **interpretive exercise (IE)** to other types with regard to some specific characteristics or use. Indicate whether test specialists would **agree (A)** or **disagree (D)** with the statements by circling the appropriate letter.

A   D   1.   The IE is more difficult to construct than other item types.

A   D   2.   The IE can be designed to measure more complex learning outcomes than the single-objective item.

A   D   3.   The IE provides a more reliable measure of complex learning outcomes than the essay test.

A   D   4.   The IE is more effective than the essay test for measuring ability to organize ideas.

A   D   5.   The IE is one of the most effective item types to use with poor readers.

A   D   6.   The IE measures knowledge of specific facts more effectively than other item types.

LEARNING GOAL: Lists the characteristics of an effective interpretive exercise.

Directions: List the important characteristics of each of the following parts of an interpretive exercise.

Introductory material:

Related test items:

(Why not have your instructor or a fellow student evaluate your items?)

Turn up bottom of page for answers

Copyright © 2000 by Merrill, an imprint of Prentice-Hall, Inc. All rights reserved.

Answers to Selection 9-A

1. A 2. A 3. A
4. D 5. D 6. D

Exercise 9-B

EVALUATING AND IMPROVING THE INTERPRETIVE EXERCISE

LEARNING GOAL: Identifies the common faults in a interpretive exercise.

Directions: Indicate the specific faults in the following interpretive exercise by circling appropriate letter (Y = yes, N = no) by each fault.

INTERPRETIVE EXERCISE

Directions: Read the paragraph and mark your answers.

Some teachers falsely believe that multiple-choice items are limited to the measurement of simple learning outcomes because they depend on the **recognition** of the answer rather than the **recall** of it. However, complex outcomes can be measured, and the selection of the correct answer is not based on the mere recognition of a previously learned answer. It involves the use of higher mental processes to arrive at a solution and then the correct answer is selected from among the alternatives presented. This is the reason multiple-choice items are also called **selection-type** items rather than **recognition-type** items. It makes clear that the answer is selected by that the mental process involved is not limited to recognition.

T	F	1.	Some teachers think multiple-choice items measure only at the recognition level.
T	F	2.	All selection-type items are recognition-type items.
T	F	3.	Multiple-choice items are also called selection-type items.
T	F	4.	Selection-type items include multiple-choice, true-false, and matching.

Items for evaluating the interpretive exercise:

Y	N	1.	Directions are adequate.
Y	N	2.	Some items measure simple reading skill only.
Y	N	3.	Some items measure extraneous material.
Y	N	4.	Some of the items can be answered without reading the paragraph.

LEARNING GOAL: Improves defective interpretive exercise.

Directions: Rewrite the directions for the above interpretive exercise and write one true-false item that calls for **interpretation** of the material.

(Why not have your instructor or a fellow student evaluate your items?)

Copyright © 2000 by Merrill, an imprint of Prentice-Hall, Inc. All rights reserved.

Answers to Selection 9-B

1. N   2. Y   3. Y   4. Y

Exercise 9-C

CONSTRUCTING INTERPRETIVE EXERCISES

LEARNING GOAL: Constructs sample exercise for interpreting a paragraph.

Directions: Construct an interpretive exercise that measure the ability to **interpret a paragraph** of written material. Include complete directions, the paragraph, and at least two multiple-choice items.

(Why not have your instructor or a fellow student evaluate your items?)

Copyright © 2000 by Merrill, an imprint of Prentice-Hall, Inc. All rights reserved.

Exercise 9-D

CONSTRUCTING INTERPRETIVE EXERCISES

LEARNING GOAL: Constructs sample exercise for interpreting pictorial material.

Directions: Construct an interpretive exercise that measures ability to **interpret a picture or cartoon**. Include complete directions, the pictorial material, and **two objective items** of any type.

(Why not have your instructor or a fellow student evaluate your items?)

Copyright © 2000 by Merrill, an imprint of Prentice-Hall, Inc. All rights reserved.

Exercise 9-E

CONSTRUCTING INTERPRETIVE EXERCISES

LEARNING GOAL: Constructs sample exercise for interpreting a table, chart, or graph.

Directions: Construct an interpretive exercise that measures ability to **interpret a table, chart, or graph**. Include complete directions, the pictorial material, and **two objective items** of any type.

(Why not have your instructor or a fellow student evaluate your items?)

Copyright © 2000 by Merrill, an imprint of Prentice-Hall, Inc. All rights reserved.

Exercise 10-A

___

CHARACTERISTICS OF ESSAY QUESTIONS

LEARNING GOAL: Identifies the advantages and limitations of essay questions in comparison to objective items.

Directions: The following statements compare **essay questions** to **objective items** with regard to some specific characteristic or use. Indicate whether test specialists would **agree (A)** or **disagree (D)** with the statement by circling the appropriate letter.

A   D   1.   Essay questions are more efficient than objective items for measuring knowledge of facts.

A   D   2.   Essay questions are more subject to bluffing than objective items.

A   D   3.   Essay questions are to be favored when measuring ability to organize.

A   D   4.   Essay questions measure a more limited sampling of content than objective questions in a given amount of testing time.

A   D   5.   Essay questions provide more reliable scores than objective items.

A   D   6.   Essay questions can measure complex learning outcomes that are difficult to measure by other means.

LEARNING GOAL: Lists the characteristics of an effective essay question.

Directions: List the important characteristics of each type of essay question.

Restricted-response question:

Extended-response question:

(Why not have your instructor or a fellow student evaluate your items?)

Copyright © 2000 by Merrill, an imprint of Prentice-Hall, Inc. All rights reserved.

Answers to Selection 10-A

1. D   2. A   3. A
4. A   5. D   6. A

Exercise 10-B

EVALUATING AND IMPROVING ESSAY QUESTIONS

LEARNING GOAL: Describes faults in essay questions and rewrites them as effective items.

Directions: Describe the faults in each of the sample essay questions and rewrite each question so that it meets the criteria for an effective essay item.

1.   Why are essay questions better than objective items?

    Faults:

    Rewrite of item:

2.   List the rules from your textbook for constructing essay questions.

    Faults:

    Rewrite of item:

3.   How do you feel about using essay questions?

    Faults:

    Rewrite of item:

4.   Write on one of the following :(1) constructing essay questions, (2) scoring essay questions, (3) using essay questions to improve learning.

    Faults:

    Rewrite of item:

(Why not have your instructor or a fellow student evaluate your items?)

Copyright © 2000 by Merrill, an imprint of Prentice-Hall, Inc. All rights reserved.

Exercise 10-C

CONSTRUCTING RESTRICTED-RESPONSE ESSAY QUESTIONS

LEARNING GOAL: Constructs sample restricted-response essay questions.

Directions: Construct one restricted-response essay question for each of the types of thought questions listed.

1.   Comparing two things.

2.   Justifying an idea or action.

3.   Classifying things or ideas.

4.   Applying a fact or principle.

(Why not have your instructor or a fellow student evaluate your items?)

Copyright © 2000 by Merrill, an imprint of Prentice-Hall, Inc. All rights reserved.

Exercise 10-D

CONSTRUCTING EXTENDED-RESPONSE ESSAY QUESTIONS

LEARNING GOAL: Constructs sample extended-response essay questions.

Directions: Construct one extended-response essay question for each of the types of thought questions listed. For each question, describe the scoring procedures to be used and the elements included in the scoring.

1. **Synthesis**: Production of a plan for doing something (e.g., experiment), for constructing something (e.g., graph, table, dress), or for taking some social action (e.g., preventing pollution).

   Question:

   Scoring procedure:

2. **Evaluation**: Judging the value for something (e.g., a proposal, a book, a poem, a teaching method, a research study) using definite criteria.

   Question:

   Scoring procedure:

(Why not have your instructor or a fellow student evaluate your items?)

Copyright © 2000 by Merrill, an imprint of Prentice-Hall, Inc. All rights reserved.

Exercise 10-E

SCORING ESSAY QUESTIONS

LEARNING GOAL: Distinguishes between good and bad practices in scoring essay questions.

Directions: Indicate whether each of the following statements describes a **good (G)** practice or a **bad (B)** practice in scoring essay questions by circling the appropriate letter.

G   B   1.   Use a model answer for scoring restricted-response questions.

G   B   2.   Evaluate all answers on a student's paper before doing the next paper.

G   B   3.   Review a student's scores on earlier tests before reading the answers.

G   B   4.   Score content and writing skills separately.

G   B   5.   Use the rating method for scoring extended-response questions.

G   B   6.   Lower the score one point for each misspelled word.

LEARNING GOAL: Prepares a list of points for scoring essay questions.

Directions: Make a list of five do's and five don'ts to serve as a guide for scoring essay tests.

DO:

1.

2.

3.

4.

5.

DON'T:

1.

2.

3.

4.

5.

(Why not have your instructor or a fellow student evaluate your items?)

Turn up bottom of page for answers

Copyright © 2000 by Merrill, an imprint of Prentice-Hall, Inc. All rights reserved.

Answers to Selection 10-E

1. G 2. B 3. B
4. G 5. G 6. B

Exercise 11-A

___

CHARACTERISTICS OF PERFORMANCE-BASED ASSESSMENT TASKS

LEARNING GOAL: Identifies the advantages and limitations of performance-based assessment tasks.

Directions: The following statements compare **performance-based assessment (PBA) tasks** to **objective items** with regard to some specific characteristic or use. Indicate whether test specialists would **agree (A)** or **disagree (D)** with the statement by circling the appropriate letter.

A   D   1.   PBA tasks are more likely to model good instruction.

A   D   2.   PBA tasks provide a better means of assessing the breadth of a student's knowledge.

A   D   3.   PBA tasks are to be favored when measuring the process that a student uses to solve a problem.

A   D   4.   PBA tasks measure a more limited sampling of behavior.

A   D   5.   PBA tasks are more suitable for measuring ability to solve ill-structured problems.

A   D   6.   PBA tasks provide more reliable scores.

LEARNING GOAL: Lists the characteristics of an effective performance-based assessment task.

Directions: List the important characteristics of each type of performance-based assessment task.

Restricted-response task:

Extended-response task:

(Why not have your instructor or a fellow student evaluate your items?)

Turn up bottom of page for answers
Copyright © 2000 by Merrill, an imprint of Prentice-Hall, Inc. All rights reserved.

Answers to Selection 11-A

1. A 2. D 3. A
4. A 5. A 6. D

Exercise 11-B

CONSTRUCTING RESTRICTED-RESPONSE PERFORMANCE-BASED ASSESSMENT TASKS

LEARNING GOAL: Constructs simple restricted-response performance-based assessment tasks.

Directions: Construct two restricted-response performance-based assessment tasks for a grade and subject matter of your choice. Include a description of the directions to students and the criteria to be used in judging the performances.

1.   Directions:

      Task:

      Scoring criteria:

2.   Directions:

      Task:

      Scoring criteria:

(Why not have your instructor or a fellow student evaluate your items?)

Copyright © 2000 by Merrill, an imprint of Prentice-Hall, Inc. All rights reserved.

Exercise 11-C

CONSTRUCTING EXTENDED-RESPONSE PERFORMANCE-BASED ASSESSMENT TASKS

LEARNING GOAL: Constructs an extended-response performance-based assessment tasks.

Directions: Construct an extended-response performance-based assessment task involving problem solving for a grade and subject matter of your choice. The task should require students to decide on an approach to solving the problem, identify or gather relevant information, and integrate that information to produce a product. Include a description of the directions to students and the criteria to be used in judging the performances.

Directions:

Task

Scoring:

(Why not have your instructor or a fellow student evaluate your items?)

Copyright © 2000 by Merrill, an imprint of Prentice-Hall, Inc. All rights reserved.

Exercise 11-D

___

RATING SCALES

LEARNING GOAL: Distinguishes between desirable and undesirable practices in using rating scales.

Directions: Indicate whether each of the following statements describes a **desirable (D)** practice or an **undesirable (U)** practice in using rating scales with performance-based assessments by circling the appropriate letter.

D   U   1.   The descriptive graphic rating scale should be favored over the numerical scale.

D   U   2.   In rating performance, derive the characteristics to be rated from the list of learning objectives.

D   U   3.   Use a least ten points on each scale to be rated.

D   U   4.   Use holistic rating procedures to provide students with diagnostic feedback.

D   U   5.   Separate ratings of secondary characteristics such as neatness, form ratings of accomplishment of primary learning objectives.

D   U   6.   Communicate the criteria to be used in judging performances to students.

LEARNING GOAL: Constructs items for a rating scale.

Directions: Prepare two items for a descriptive graphic rating scale to be used in assessing some type of student performance or some product produced by the student. Do not use sample items from your textbook.

(Why not have your instructor or a fellow student evaluate your items?)

Turn up bottom of page for answers
Copyright © 2000 by Merrill, an imprint of Prentice-Hall, Inc. All rights reserved.

Answers to Selection 11-D

1. D   2. D   3. U
4. U   5. D   6. D

Exercise 11-E

CHECKLISTS

LEARNING GOAL: Distinguishes between desirable and undesirable practices in using checklists.

Directions: Indicate whether each of the following statements describes a **desirable (D)** practice or an **undesirable (U)** practice in using checklists by circling the appropriate letter.

D   U   1.   Use a checklist wherever frequency of occurrence is an important element in the assessment.

D   U   2.   In assessing performance, include in a checklist both desired actions and common errors.

D   U   3.   Use a checklist for assessing some products.

D   U   4.   Use a checklist to determine if steps in performance were completed in proper order.

D   U   5.   Use a checklist for assessing process but not for assessing student products.

D   U   6.   Avoid use of checklists in assessing process.

LEARNING GOAL: Constructs a performance checklist.

Directions: Prepare a brief checklist for some simple performance-based assessment task. Include directions describing how to respond.

(Why not have your instructor or a fellow student evaluate your items?)

Copyright © 2000 by Merrill, an imprint of Prentice-Hall, Inc. All rights reserved.

Answers to Selection 11-E

1. U   2. D   3. D
4. D   5. U   6. U

Exercise 12-A

PURPOSES

LEARNING GOAL: Identifies and distinguishes among the major purposes of portfolios.

Directions: The poles of four dimensions distinguishing the purposes of portfolios are listed below. Describe the ways in which the purposes of portfolios at the ends of each continuum differ.

1.   a.   Instruction

     b.   Assessment

2.   a.   Current accomplishments

     b.   Progress

3.   a. Showcase

     b.   Documentation

4.   a.   Finished

     b.   Working

(Why not have your instructor or a fellow student evaluate your items?)

Copyright © 2000 by Merrill, an imprint of Prentice-Hall, Inc. All rights reserved.

Exercise 12-B

STRENGTHS AND WEAKNESSES

LEARNING GOAL: Identifies major strengths and weaknesses of using portfolios of student work for particular purposes.

Directions: Identify four strengths and three weaknesses of portfolios when used for purposes of assessment.

Strengths:

1.

2.

3.

4.

Weaknesses:

1.

2.

3.

(Why not have your instructor or a fellow student evaluate your items?)

Copyright © 2000 by Merrill, an imprint of Prentice-Hall, Inc. All rights reserved.

Exercise 12-C

GUIDELINES FOR PORTFOLIO ENTRIES

LEARNING GOAL: Constructs sample guidelines for entries in a portfolio designed for a specified assessment purpose.

Directions: Construct sample guidelines for entries in a portfolio dealing with each of the four issues below assuming that the portfolio is intended for assessing a student's progress in writing during the school year.

Guidelines of Uses of Portfolio:

Guidelines Regarding Access to Portfolio:

Guidelines on Portfolio Construction and Entries:

Guidelines on the Criteria for Evaluation of the Portfolio:

(Why not have your instructor or a fellow student evaluate your items?)

Copyright © 2000 by Merrill, an imprint of Prentice-Hall, Inc. All rights reserved.

Exercise 12-D

EVALUATION CRITERIA

LEARNING GOAL: Identifies characteristics of effective criteria for evaluating student portfolios.

Directions: Indicate whether measurement specialists would **agree (A)** or **disagree (D)** with each of the following statements concerning current trends in testing and assessment by circling the appropriate letter.

A   D   1.   Fairness is enhanced by clear specifications of evaluation criteria.

A   D   2.   Reliability of scores assigned to portfolios is enhanced by using holistic evaluation criteria for the portfolio as a whole rather than criteria for individual entries.

A   D   3.   It is desirable for students to include self evaluations of their work with their portfolio entries.

A   D   4.   Analytic criteria are more useful for summative evaluations than for formative evaluations of portfolio entries.

A   D   5.   Evaluation criteria should be communicated to students in the guidelines provided to students for constructing their portfolios.

A   D   6.   Evaluation criteria, while necessary for portfolios used for assessment purposes, are not needed for portfolios used for instructional purposes.

LEARNING GOAL: Constructs evaluation criteria for entries in a portfolio used to display best works.

Directions: Construct a set of evaluation criteria to be used for a portfolio designed to be a showcase of a student's best work in a subject area of interest to you.

(Why not have your instructor or a fellow student evaluate your items?)

Copyright © 2000 by Merrill, an imprint of Prentice-Hall, Inc. All rights reserved.

Answers to Selection 12-D

1. A   2. D   3. A
4. D   5. A   6. D

Exercise 12-E

PORTFOLIO CONSTRUCTION

LEARNING GOAL: Constructs a showcase portfolio for a class

Directions: For a class of your choice, construct a showcase portfolio to demonstrate your best work in that subject area.

(Why not have your instructor or a fellow student evaluate your items?)

Copyright © 2000 by Merrill, an imprint of Prentice-Hall, Inc. All rights reserved.

Exercise 13-A

ANECDOTAL RECORDS

LEARNING GOAL: Distinguishes between desirable and undesirable practices in using anecdotal records.

Directions: Indicate whether each of the following statements describes a **desirable (D)** practice or an **undesirable (U)** practice in using anecdotal records by circling the appropriate letter.

D   U   1.   Confine observations to areas that can be verified by objective testing.

D   U   2.   Keep factual descriptions of incidents and interpretations of them separate.

D   U   3.   Limit each anecdote to a single incident.

D   U   4.   Limit each anecdote to the behavior of only one student.

D   U   5.   Wait until after school hours to record the observed incidents.

D   U   6.   Record both positive and negative incidents.

LEARNING GOAL: Writes an anecdotal record on an incident.

Directions: Briefly observe some aspect of student performance (e.g., speaking, playing a game) and write an anecdotal record of the incident.

(Why not have your instructor or a fellow student evaluate your items?)

Turn up bottom of page for answers

Copyright © 2000 by Merrill, an imprint of Prentice-Hall, Inc. All rights reserved.

Answers to Selection 13-A

1. U 2. D 3. D
4. U 5. U 6. D

Exercise 13-B

USE OF PEER APPRAISAL AND SELF-REPORT TECHNIQUES

LEARNING GOAL: Selects the most appropriate technique for a particular use.

Directions: Indicate which technique is **most appropriate** for each of the uses listed below by circling the appropriate letter.

      KEY G = "Guess who" technique, S = Sociometric technique,
            A = Attitude scale, I = Interest inventory

G   S   A   I   1.   To analyze the social structure of a group.

G   S   A   I   2.   To aid in selection reading material for a poor reader.

G   S   A   I   3.   To determine the reputation a student holds among his or her classmates.

G   S   A   I   4.   To aid in assessing the effectiveness of instructional activities.

G   S   A   I   5.   To determine how well a particular student is accepted by his or her classmates.

G   S   A   I   6.   To aid students in career planning.

LEARNING GOAL: States the advantages and disadvantages of peer appraisal and self-report techniques.

Directions: Briefly state **one advantage** and **one disadvantage** of each of the following techniques.

Peer appraisal:

Self report:

(Why not have your instructor or a fellow student evaluate your items?)

Turn up **bottom of page** for answers
Copyright © 2000 by Merrill, an imprint of Prentice-Hall, Inc. All rights reserved.

Answers to Selection 13-B

1. S 2. I 3. G
4. A 5. S 6. I

Exercise 13-C

GUESS WHO TECHNIQUE

LEARNING GOAL: Distinguishes between desirable and undesirable practices in using the guess who technique.

Directions: Indicate whether each of the following statements describes a **desirable (D)** practice or an **undesirable (U)** practice in using the guess who techniques by circling the appropriate letter.

D　　U　　1.　　Use only clearly favorable behavior descriptions.

D　　U　　2.　　Have students write as many names as they wish for each behavior description.

D　　U　　3.　　Permit students to name a person for more than one behavior description.

D　　U　　4.　　Have students respond by using first name and initial of last name.

D　　U　　5.　　Use the guess who technique for evaluation personal and social development only.

D　　U　　6.　　Score the responses by counting the number of nominations a student receives on each behavior description.

LEARNING GOAL: Constructs items for a guess who form.

Directions: List six statements that could be used in a guess who form for evaluating students "study and work habits."

(Why not have your instructor or a fellow student evaluate your items?)

Turn up bottom of page for answers
Copyright © 2000 by Merrill, an imprint of Prentice-Hall, Inc. All rights reserved.

Answers to Selection 13-C

1. U   2. D   3. D
4. D   5. U   6. D

Exercise 13-D

SOCIOMETRIC TECHNIQUE

LEARNING GOAL: Distinguishes between desirable and undesirable practices in using the sociometric technique.

Directions: Indicate whether each of the following statements describes a **desirable (D)** practice or and **undesirable (U)** practice in using the sociometric technique by circling the appropriate letter.

D   U   1.   Sociometric choices should be real choices that are actually used to arrange groups.

D   U   2.   The situations used in sociometric choosing should be ones in which all students are equally free to participate.

D   U   3.   Students should be told to state their first choice **only**, in order to simplify the tabulation of results.

D   U   4.   The plotted sociogram should show the social position of each student and the social pattern of the group.

D   U   5.   Each student should be shown, in an individual conference, his or her place on the sociogram.

D   U   6.   Sociometric choices should be used to assess the influence of school practices on students' social relations.

LEARNING GOAL: Constructs items for a sociometric form.

Directions: List three choice situations to be used on a sociometric form. The situations should be suitable for the grade level at which it is to be used. Indicate the grade level. Do not use any sample items from your textbook.

(Why not have your instructor or a fellow student evaluate your items?)

Copyright © 2000 by Merrill, an imprint of Prentice-Hall, Inc. All rights reserved.

Answers to Selection 13-D

1. D 2. D 3. U
4. D 5. U 6. D

Exercise 13-E

ATTITUDE MEASUREMENT

LEARNING GOAL: Distinguishes between desirable and undesirable practices in using a Likert-type attitude scale.

Directions: Indicate whether each of the following statements describes a **desirable (D)** practice or an **undesirable (U)** practice in using a Likert-type attitude scale by circling the appropriate letter.

D   U   1.   Use only clearly favorable and unfavorable attitude statements.

D   U   2.   Have students write statements for use in the attitude scale.

D   U   3.   Arrange the statements in the scale in order, from least favorable to most favorable.

D   U   4.   Have students respond by indicating how strongly they agree or disagree.

D   U   5.   Use a group of judges to obtain scoring weights.

D   U   6.   Have students put their names on the attitude scale.

LEARNING GOAL: Constructs a Likert-type attitude scale.

Directions: List six statements that could be used to measure student attitudes toward **testing** according to a Likert-type scale. Include a place to respond and the scoring weights for each item.

(Why not have your instructor or a fellow student evaluate your items?)

Copyright © 2000 by Merrill, an imprint of Prentice-Hall, Inc. All rights reserved.

Answers to Selection 13-E

1. D   2. D   3. U
4. D   5. U   6. U

Exercise 14-A

REVIEWING AND ARRANGING ITEMS AND TASKS IN CLASSROOM TESTS AND ASSESSMENTS

LEARNING GOAL: Distinguishes between good and bad practices in reviewing and arranging test items and assessment tasks.

Directions: Indicate whether each of the following statements describes a **good (G)** practice or a **bad (B)** practice in reviewing items and tasks and arranging them in classroom tests and assessments by circling the appropriate letter.

G   B   1.   Have another teacher review the items and tasks for defects.

G   B   2.   Recheck relevance to the specific learning outcome when reviewing an item or task.

G   B   3.   During item and task review, remove any racial or sexual stereotyping.

G   B   4.   In arranging items in the test, place essay questions or other performance tasks first.

G   B   5.   Intersperse true-false items among multiple-choice items.

G   B   6.   Put easy items last to maintain student motivation.

LEARNING GOAL: Prepares a list of points for reviewing and arranging test items and assessment tasks.

Directions: Make a list of **four do's** and **four don'ts** to serve as a guide for reviewing and arranging test items and assessment tasks.

DO
1.

2.

3.

4.

DON'T
1.

2.

3.

4.

(Why not have your instructor or a fellow student evaluate your items?)

Copyright © 2000 by Merrill, an imprint of Prentice-Hall, Inc. All rights reserved.

Answers to Selection 14-A

1. G 2. G 3. G
4. B 5. B 6. B

Exercise 14-B

PREPARING TEST DIRECTIONS

LEARNING GOAL: Prepares sample directions for a classroom test.

Directions: Prepare a complete set of directions for a test in some subject. Assume that the general directions for the test as a whole and the specific directions for each item type are all for the same test.

General directions:

Short-answer items:

True-false items:

Multiple-choice items:

Matching items:

(Why not have your instructor or a fellow student evaluate your items?)

Copyright © 2000 by Merrill, an imprint of Prentice-Hall, Inc. All rights reserved.

Exercise 14-C

ADMINISTERING AND SCORING CLASSROOM TESTS AND ASSESSMENTS

LEARNING GOAL: Distinguishes between good and bad practice in administering and scoring classroom tests and assessments.

Directions: Indicate whether each of the following statements describes a **good (G)** practice or a **bad (B)** practice in administering and scoring classroom tests and assessments by circling the appropriate letter.

G   B   1.   Students are told whether there is a correction for guessing.

G   B   2.   Students answer every item, so their scores are corrected for guessing.

G   B   3.   Students are told how much time to spend on each part of the test and each extended response task.

G   B   4.   Students are told to skip items that seem too difficult and come back to them later.

G   B   5.   The teacher explains the meaning of an ambiguous question to the student who asked about it.

G   B   6.   An objective test is scored by counting important items 1 point and very important items 2 points.

LEARNING GOAL: Describes and illustrates use of the correction-for-guessing formula.

Directions: Describe when the correction-for-guessing formula should and should not be used for classroom tests and compare the corrected scores for the given data.

Use the correction formula when:

Do not use the correction formula when:

Compute the corrected scores on an eight-item, true-false test for the student responses shown below:
    (R = Right, W = Wrong, O = Omit)

	1	2	3	4	5	6	7	8	Corrected Score
Bob	R	R	R	R	R	R	O	O	
Sara	R	R	R	R	R	W	R	W	
Terry	R	R	R	W	O	R	W	W	

(Why not have your instructor or a fellow student evaluate your items?)

Turn up bottom of page for answers
Copyright © 2000 by Merrill, an imprint of Prentice-Hall, Inc. All rights reserved.

Answers to Selection 14-C

1. G   2. B   3. G
4. G   5. B   6. B
Bob, 6; Sara, 4; Terry, 1

Exercise 14-D

___

ITEM ANALYSIS PROCEDURES FOR NORM-REFERENCED CLASSROOM TESTS

LEARNING GOAL: Computes and interprets item analyses.

Directions: Review the following item analysis data and answer the questions below the data. For each item their are 10 students in the upper group and 10 students in the lower group. The data indicate the number of students choosing each alternative. The correct answer is marked (*).

Item number		Alternatives			
		A	B	C	D
1.	Upper	*10	0	0	0
	Lower	2	2	3	3
2.	Upper	0	1	*8	1
	Lower	5	1	*3	1
3.	Upper	2	*5	2	1
	Lower	3	*4	2	1
4.	Upper	*6	2	1	1
	Lower	*2	3	2	3
5.	Upper	3	0	0	*7
	Lower	0	4	5	*1

1. What is the **difficulty** of item 2? _____

2. What is the **discriminating** power of item 2? _____

3. Which one of the above items is **most** discriminating? _____

4. Which one of the above items is **least** discriminating? _____

5. Which one of the above items has a **negatively** discriminating distracter? _____

6. Which one of the above items most closely meets **all** the criteria for and ideal item? _____

List the cautions in interpreting item analysis results like the above.

(Why not have your instructor or a fellow student evaluate your items?)

Copyright © 2000 by Merrill, an imprint of Prentice-Hall, Inc. All rights reserved.

Answers to Selection 14-D

1. 55% 2. .50 3. 1
4. 3   5. 5   6. 1

Exercise 14-E

APPLICATION OF ITEM ANALYSIS PRINCIPLES TO PERFORMANCE-BASED ASSESSMENT TASKS

LEARNING GOAL: Applies and interprets item analysis principles with performance-based assessment tasks.

Directions: A set of eight performance-based assessment tasks were administered to a group of 30 students. Each task was scored on a five-point scale. The total score for the assessment was the sum of the eight task scores. Total scores for the assessment and scores on the last task of the assessment are listed below. The scores are listed in order of the total score. Use these data to analyze the discriminating power of last task by comparing the performance of the upper and lower groups of ten students.

Student	1	2	3	4	5	6	7	8	9	10
Total Score	36	35	35	34	33	33	33	32	32	32
Score on Item 8	5	5	4	5	4	4	4	3	5	3

Student	11	12	13	14	15	16	17	18	19	20
Total Score	31	30	30	30	29	29	29	29	28	28
Score on Item 8	4	4	3	3	4	3	3	3	3	2

Student	21	22	23	24	25	26	27	28	29	30
Total Score	27	27	26	25	23	23	21	20	18	16
Score on Item 8	4	3	3	3	3	2	3	2	1	1

Construct an analysis table for Item 8

Briefly interpret the results of your analysis.

(Why not have your instructor or a fellow student evaluate your items?)

Turn up bottom of page for answers
Copyright © 2000 by Merrill, an imprint of Prentice-Hall, Inc. All rights reserved.

Answers to Selection 14-E

Score	1	2	3	4	5	Average
Upper	0	0	2	4	4	4.2
Lower	2	2	5	1	0	2.5

Exercise 15-A

TYPES OF MARKING AND REPORTING SYSTEMS

LEARNING GOAL: Distinguishes among the characteristics of different types of marking and reporting systems.

Directions: Indicate which type of marking and reporting system best fits each statement listed below by circling the appropriate letter, using the following key.

> KEY: A = traditional letter grade (A,B,C,D,F), B = Two-letter grade (pass, fail),
> C = Checklist of objectives, D = Parent-teacher conference.

A   B   C   D   1.   Provides for two-way reporting.

A   B   C   D   2.   Provides most useful learning guide to student.

A   B   C   D   3.   Provides least information concerning learning.

A   B   C   D   4.   Most preferred by college admissions officers.

A   B   C   D   5.   May be too complex to be understood by parents.

A   B   C   D   6.   Most widely used method of reporting in high school.

LEARNING GOAL: Lists the advantages and disadvantages of the traditional (A,B,C,D,F) marking system.

Directions: List the advantages and disadvantages of using the traditional (A,B,C,D,F) marking system as the **sole** method of reporting student progress.

Advantages:

Disadvantages:

(Why not have your instructor or a fellow student evaluate your items?)

Turn up bottom of page for answers

Copyright © 2000 by Merrill, an imprint of Prentice-Hall, Inc. All rights reserved.

Answers to Selection 15-A

1. D   2. C   3. B
4. A   5. C   6. A

Exercise 15-B

ASSIGNING RELATIVE LETTER GRADES

LEARNING GOAL: Distinguishes between desirable and undesirable practices in assigning relative letter grades.

Directions: Indicate whether each of the following statements describes a **desirable (D)** practice or an **undesirable (U)** practice in assigning relative letter grades by circling the appropriate letter.

D   U   1.   The grades should reflect the learning outcomes specified for the course.

D   U   2.   To give test scores equal weight in a composite score, the scores should be simply added together.

D   U   3.   If it is decided to assign different weights to some scores, the weighting should be based on the maximum possible score on the test.

D   U   4.   Grades should be lowered for tardiness or misbehavior.

D   U   5.   Grading typically should be based on the normal curve.

D   U   6.   Pass-fail decisions should be based on an absolute standard of achievement.

LEARNING GOAL: Assigns weights in obtaining composite scores for grading purposes.

Directions: Following is a list of types of information a teacher would like to include in assigning a final grade to each student. If the teacher wants to count each type of information one-fourth of the final grade, what weight should be given to each type of information?

Type of Information	Range of Scores	Weight to Be Used
Midsemester examination	30 to 50	
Term project	5 to 10	
Performance assessments	15 to 25	
Final examination	20 to 100	

(Why not have your instructor or a fellow student evaluate your items?)

Copyright © 2000 by Merrill, an imprint of Prentice-Hall, Inc. All rights reserved.

Answers to Selection 15-B

1. D 2. U 3. U
4. U 5. U 6. D
Weights: 4, 16, 8, 1

Exercise 15-C

ASSIGNING ABSOLUTE GRADES

LEARNING GOAL: Distinguishes between desirable and undesirable practices in assigning absolute grades.

Directions: Indicate whether each of the following statements describes a **desirable (D)** practice or an **undesirable (U)** practice in assigning absolute letter grades by circling the appropriate letter.

D   U   1.   Absolute grades should be used with mastery learning.

D   U   2.   Clearly defined domains of learning tasks should provide the basis for grading.

D   U   3.   If all students pass a test, a harder test should be given before grades are assigned.

D   U   4.   The distribution of grades to be assigned should be predetermined and explained.

D   U   5.   Grades should be based on the amount of improvement shown.

D   U   6.   When using absolute grading the standard for passing should be predetermined.

LEARNING GOAL: Lists guidelines for effective grading.

Directions: List five important guidelines for effective grading.

1.

2.

3.

4.

5.

(Why not have your instructor or a fellow student evaluate your items?)

Copyright © 2000 by Merrill, an imprint of Prentice-Hall, Inc. All rights reserved.

Answers to Selection 15-C

1. D 2. D 3. U
4. U 5. U 6. D

Exercise 15-D

PARENT-TEACHER CONFERENCE

LEARNING GOAL: Distinguishes between desirable and undesirable practices in conducting a parent-teacher conference.

Directions: Indicate whether each of the following statements describes a **desirable (D)** practice or an **undesirable (U)** practice in conducting parent-teacher conferences by circling the appropriate letter.

D   U   1.   Before the conference, assemble a portfolio of specific information about and examples of the student's learning progress.

D   U   2.   Present examples of the student's work to parents

D   U   3.   Begin the conference by describing the student's learning difficulties.

D   U   4.   Make clear to parents that, as a teacher, you know what is best for the student's learning and development.

D   U   5.   In the concluding phase, review your conference notes with the parents.

D   U   6.   End the conference with a positive comment about the student.

LEARNING GOAL: Lists questions that might be asked of parents during the conference.

Directions: Write a list of questions that you could ask parents during a conference that might help you better understand students' problems of learning and development.

(Why not have your instructor or a fellow student evaluate your items?)

Copyright © 2000 by Merrill, an imprint of Prentice-Hall, Inc. All rights reserved.

Answers to Selection 15-D

1. D 2. D 3. U
4. U 5. D 6. D

Exercise 15-E

___

REPORTING RESULTS OF PUBLISHED TESTS TO PARENTS

LEARNING GOAL: Distinguishes between desirable and undesirable practices in reporting results of published tests to parents.

Directions: Indicate whether each of the following statements describes a **desirable (D)** practice or an **undesirable (U)** practice in reporting results of published tests to parents by circling the appropriate letter.

D   U   1.   Describe what the test measures in brief, understandable terms.

D   U   2.   Make clear the distinction between percentile rank and percentage-correct scores.

D   U   3.   Use grade equivalent scores to indicate the grade at which the student can perform.

D   U   4.   Use the same type of score to report all test results, whenever possible.

D   U   5.   Describe a difference between two test scores as a "real difference" only after the error of measurement is considered.

D   U   6.   Explain how the test results will be used only if the parent asks.

LEARNING GOAL: Identifies and corrects common errors in reporting standardized test results.

Directions: Indicate what is wrong with each of the following statements and rewrite each one so that it provides an accurate report.

1.   "Derek's percentile rank of 70 in spelling means he can spell 70 percent of the words in the test."

2.   "Marie's stanine score of 6 in reading indicates she is perform below average in reading."

3.   "Erik's grade-equivalent scores of 5.4 in reading and 6.2 in math indicate that his performance in math is superior to his performance in reading."

(Why not have your instructor or a fellow student evaluate your items?)

Turn up bottom of page for answers
Copyright © 2000 by Merrill, an imprint of Prentice-Hall, Inc. All rights reserved.

Answers to Selection 15-E

1. D 2. D 3. U
4. D 5. D 6. U

Exercise 16-A

STANDARDIZED ACHIEVEMENT TESTS VERSUS INFORMAL CLASSROOM TESTS

LEARNING GOAL: Identifies the comparative advantages of standardized and informal classroom tests for measuring student achievement.

Directions: Indicate whether each of the following statements best describes a **standardized** achievement test **(S)** or an informal **classroom** test **(C)** by circling the appropriate letter.

S   C   1.   Likely to be more relevant to a teacher's instructional objectives.

S   C   2.   Likely to provide more reliable test scores.

S   C   3.   Technical quality of test items is consistently high.

S   C   4.   Most useful in formative assessment.

S   C   5.   Typically provides the larger spread of scores.

S   C   6.   Best for use in rapidly changing content areas.

LEARNING GOAL: States a major advantage and limitation of standardized achievement tests.

Directions: Briefly state one major advantage and one major limitation of standardized achievement tests.

Advantage:

Limitation:

(Why not have your instructor or a fellow student evaluate your items?)

Copyright © 2000 by Merrill, an imprint of Prentice-Hall, Inc. All rights reserved.

Answers to Selection 16-A

1. C   2. S   3. S
4. C   5. S   6. C

Exercise 16-B

USE OF PUBLISHED ACHIEVEMENT TEST BATTERIES

LEARNING GOAL: Selects the most appropriate type of achievement test battery for a particular use.

Directions: Indicate which type of test is most useful for each of the following testing purposes by circling the appropriate letter using the following key.

KEY   S = Survey achievement test battery
           D = Diagnostic achievement test battery

S   D   1.   To compare schools on basic skill development.

S   D   2.   To describe the specific skills a student has yet to learn in reading.

S   D   3.   To measure achievement in science and social studies.

S   D   4.   To detect specific weaknesses in adding fractions.

S   D   5.   To determine how a fifth-grade class compares to other fifth grade classes in reading.

S   D   6.   To determine mastery of particular language skills.

LEARNING GOAL: States a major advantage and limitation of achievement test batteries.

Directions: Briefly state one major advantage and one major limitation of achievement test batteries of the **survey** type.

Advantage:

Limitation:

(Why not have your instructor or a fellow student evaluate your items?)

Turn up bottom of page for answers
Copyright © 2000 by Merrill, an imprint of Prentice-Hall, Inc. All rights reserved.

Answers to Selection 16-B

1. S 2. D 3. S
4. D 5. S 6. D

Exercise 16-C

___

COMPARISON OF READING READINESS TESTS AND READING SURVEY TESTS

LEARNING GOAL: Identifies the functions measured by different types of reading tests.

Directions: Indicate whether each of the functions listed below is measured by reading **readiness** tests **(R)**, by reading **survey** tests **(S)**, by **both (B)**, or by **neither (N)**, by circling the appropriate letter.

R   S   B   N   1.   Auditory discrimination.

R   S   B   N   2.   Comprehension of the meaning of words.

R   S   B   N   3.   Ability to draw inferences.

R   S   B   N   4.   Ability to read maps.

R   S   B   N   5.   Rate of reading.

R   S   B   N   6.   Attitude toward reading.

LEARNING GOAL: Compares reading tests.

Directions: Compare two reading survey tests (or readiness tests) for a particular grade level (1) briefly describe how the two tests differ, and (2) indicate which one you would prefer to use for a particular purpose and why.

(Why not have your instructor or a fellow student evaluate your items?)

Copyright © 2000 by Merrill, an imprint of Prentice-Hall, Inc. All rights reserved.

Answers to Selection 16-C

1. R   2. B   3. S
4. N   5. S   6. N

Exercise 16-D

COMPARISON OF STANDARDIZED AND CUSTOMIZED ACHIEVEMENT TESTS

LEARNING GOAL: Distinguishes among the characteristics of different types of achievement tests.

Directions: Indicate which type of test best fits each feature listed below by circling the appropriate letter, using the following key.

KEY: S = Standardized Achievement Tests
           C = Customized Achievement Tests

S   C   1.   Are most useful to the classroom teacher.

S   C   2.   Have the greatest need for adequate norms.

S   C   3.   Most adaptable to changing conditions.

S   C   4.   Most likely to have some content the students have not studied.

S   C   5.   Best for making criterion-referenced interpretations.

S   C   6.   Likely to provide the most valid measure of local instructional objectives.

LEARNING GOAL: Describes the procedure for producing customized achievement tests.

Directions: List and briefly describe the procedural steps to follow in producing locally prepared customized achievement tests.

(Why not have your instructor or a fellow student evaluate your items?)

Turn up bottom of page for answers
Copyright © 2000 by Merrill, an imprint of Prentice-Hall, Inc. All rights reserved.

Answers to Selection 16-D

1. C   2. S   3. C
4. S   5. C   6. C

Exercise 16-E

SELECTING PUBLISHED ACHIEVEMENT TESTS

LEARNING GOAL: Selects the type of test that is most appropriate for a particular purpose.

Directions: For each of the following statements, indicate which type of test would be used by circling the appropriate letter using the following key.

KEY: A = Achievement Test Battery, B = Separate Test of Content,
     C = Customized Achievement Test, D = Individual Achievement Test

A   B   C   D   1.   To test student's mastery of classroom objectives.

A   B   C   D   2.   To test a student who has a learning disability.

A   B   C   D   3.   To compare a student's performance in reading and mathematics.

A   B   C   D   4.   To test students at the end of each unit.

A   B   C   D   5.   To determine how a classroom final examination in science compares to a standardized test.

A   B   C   D   6.   To measure student progress from one grade level to the next.

LEARNING GOAL: Compares the usefulness of customized tests and standardized tests.

Directions: State one advantage and one disadvantage of using a customized test instead of a standardized test to measure student achievement.

Advantage:

Disadvantage:

(Why not have your instructor or a fellow student evaluate your items?)

Copyright © 2000 by Merrill, an imprint of Prentice-Hall, Inc. All rights reserved.

Answers to Selection 16-E

1. C   2. D   3. A
4. C   5. B   6. A

Exercise 17-A

COMPARISON OF APTITUDE AND ACHIEVEMENT TESTS

LEARNING GOAL: Identifies the similarities and differences in the characteristics of aptitude and achievement tests.

Directions: Indicate whether each of the following statements is characteristic of an **aptitude (P)** test, an **achievement (C)** test, or **both (B)** types of tests by circling the appropriate letter.

P   C   B   1.   Measures learned ability.

P   C   B   2.   Useful in predicting future achievement.

P   C   B   3.   Content-related evidence of validity is emphasized.

P   C   B   4.   Criterion-related evidence of validity is emphasized.

P   C   B   5.   Can be used in grades from kindergarten through grade 12.

P   C   B   6.   Emphasizes reasoning abilities.

LEARNING GOAL: Lists the major differences between aptitude and achievement tests.

Directions: List the **major differences** between aptitude tests and achievement tests.

(Why not have your instructor or a fellow student evaluate your items?)

Turn up bottom of page for answers
Copyright © 2000 by Merrill, an imprint of Prentice-Hall, Inc. All rights reserved.

Answers to Selection 17-A

1. B   2. B   3. C
4. P   5. B   6. P

Exercise 17-B

GROUP TESTS OF LEARNING ABILITY

LEARNING GOAL: Identifies the types of scores provided by selected group tests.

Directions: Indicate the types of scores provided by each of the group tests listed below by circling the appropriate letter using the following key
        KEY: A = single score, B = verbal and quantitative scores only,
              C = verbal, nonverbal and total scores only,
              D = verbal, quantitative, and nonverbal scores, E = more than three scores.

A   B   C   D   E   1.   Cognitive Abilities Test.

A   B   C   D   E   2.   Differential Aptitude Tests.

A   B   C   D   E   3.   Matrix Analogies Test.

A   B   C   D   E   4.   Otis-Lennon School Ability Test.

LEARNING GOAL: States advantages and disadvantages of using different types of learning ability tests.

Directions: Briefly state one advantage and one disadvantage of each type of group test of learning ability.

Single score.

Separate-scores (verbal, nonverbal, quantitative).

(Why not have your instructor or a fellow student evaluate your items?)

Turn up bottom of page for answers
Copyright © 2000 by Merrill, an imprint of Prentice-Hall, Inc. All rights reserved.

Answers to Selection 17-B

1. D   2. E   3. A   4. C

Exercise 17-C

INDIVIDUAL TESTS

LEARNING GOAL: Identifies the similarities and differences in the characteristics of individual tests.

Directions: Indicate whether each of the following statements is characteristic of the <u>Stanford-Binet Intelligence Scale</u> **(S)**, the <u>Wechsler Intelligence Scales-Revised</u> **(W)**, or **both (B)**.

S   W   B   1.   Uses a variety of item types.

S   W   B   2.   Items are arranged by subtest.

S   W   B   3.   Includes a vocabulary test.

S   W   B   4.   Provides separate verbal and performance IQs.

S   W   B   5.   Scores are reported in Standard Age Scores.

S   W   B   6.   Provides total scores and scores on subtests.

LEARNING GOAL: List conditions that might lower scores on tests of learning abilities.

Directions: List five conditions that might lower a student's score on a test of learning ability.

1.

2.

3.

4.

5.

(Why not have your instructor or a fellow student evaluate your items?)

Copyright © 2000 by Merrill, an imprint of Prentice-Hall, Inc. All rights reserved.

Answers to Selection 17-C

1. B   2. B   3. B
4. W   5. S   6. B

Exercise 17-D

DIFFERENTIAL APTITUDE TESTING

LEARNING GOAL: Identifies the characteristics of the Differential Aptitude Tests (DAT).

Directions: Indicate whether each of the following statements is characteristic of the Differential Aptitude Tests (DAT) by circling **yes** (if it is) and **no** (if it is not).

Yes   No   1.   The DAT would be classified as a test battery.

Yes   No   2.   The intercorrelations between subtests on the DAT are high (average about .90).

Yes   No   3.   Some of the DAT subtests measure abilities like those measured by group scholastic aptitude tests.

Yes   No   4.   The DAT profile indicates scores in terms of percentile rank.

Yes   No   5.   The DAT can be administered "adaptively".

Yes   No   6.   The eight tests on the DAT are speed tests.

LEARNING GOAL: States a major advantage and limitation of the Differential Aptitude Tests.

Directions: Briefly state one major advantage and one major limitation of using the Differential Aptitude Tests instead of a series of separate tests from different publishers.

Advantage of DAT:

Limitation of DAT:

(Why not have your instructor or a fellow student evaluate your items?)

Copyright © 2000 by Merrill, an imprint of Prentice-Hall, Inc. All rights reserved.

Answers to Selection 17-D

1. Y 2. N 3. Y
4. Y 5. Y 6. N

Exercise 17-E

SELECTING APPROPRIATE TESTS

LEARNING GOAL: Selects the type of test that is most appropriate for a particular use.

Directions: For each of the following purposes indicate which type of test should be used by circling the appropriate letter, using the following key.

KEY: G = Group test of learning ability, I = Individual test of learning ability,
        D = Differential aptitude tests.

G   I   D   1.   To test a preschool child.

G   I   D   2.   To test a fourth-grade student who is unable to speak.

G   I   D   3.   To test a sixth-grade student who has a severe learning disability.

G   I   D   4.   To assist a tenth-grade student with career planning.

G   I   D   5.   To aid forming learning groups within the classroom.

G   I   D   6.   To aid in planning an individual program for students with severe learning disabilities.

LEARNING GOAL: Compares the usefulness of culture-fair test and conventional test of learning ability.

Directions: State one advantage and one disadvantage of using a culture-fair test instead of a conventional learning ability test for testing students from disadvantaged homes.

Advantage:

Disadvantage:

(Why not have your instructor or a fellow student evaluate your items?)

Turn up bottom of page for answers
Copyright © 2000 by Merrill, an imprint of Prentice-Hall, Inc. All rights reserved.

Answers to Selection 17-E

1. I   2. G   3. I
4. D   5. G   6. I

Exercise 18-A

_____

SOURCES OF INFORMATION ON PUBLISHED TESTS

LEARNING GOAL: Identifies the most useful source of information for a given situation.

Directions: Below is a list of four sources of information concerning published tests. For each of the statements following the list, indicate the source of information that should be consulted **first** by circling the appropriate letter.

> KEY   A = Mental Measurements Yearbooks, B = Professional journals,
>   C = Test manual, D = Test publisher's catalog.

A   B   C   D   1.   To locate the most recent tests in an area.

A   B   C   D   2.   To obtain critical reviews of a published test.

A   B   C   D   3.   To find out how a particular published test was constructed.

A   B   C   D   4.   To locate the most recent research studies using a particular test.

A   B   C   D   5.   To determine if any tests of study skills have been published.

A   B   C   D   6.   To determine the type of norms used in a published test.

LEARNING GOAL: Summarizes the purpose and content of the <u>Standards for Educational and Psychological Testing</u>.

Directions: Briefly describe the purpose and content of the <u>Standards for Educational and Psychological Testing</u>.

Purpose:

Content:

(Why not have your instructor or a fellow student evaluate your items?)

Copyright © 2000 by Merrill, an imprint of Prentice-Hall, Inc. All rights reserved.

Answers to Selection 18-A

1. D   2. A   3. C
4. B   5. A   6. C

Exercise 18-B

___

EVALUATING AN ACHIEVEMENT TEST

LEARNING GOAL: Evaluates a test using a test evaluation form.

Directions: Select an achievement test at the grade level of your choice and obtain a copy of the test, the manual, and other accessory material; your instructor can help you with this. Study the test materials, consult the reviews in the latest <u>Mental Measurements Yearbook</u> (MMY) and <u>Test Critiques</u>, and write your evaluation using the following test evaluation form. Be brief and include only the most essential information.

TEST EVALUATION FORM

Test title _____ Author(s)_____

Publisher _____ Copyright date(s) _____

Purpose of test _____

For grades (ages)_____ Forms _____

Scores available _____ Method of scoring _____

Administration time_____ Time(s) of parts _____

Validity (cite manual pages) _____. Summarize evidence below.

Content considerations:

Test-criterion relationships:

Construct considerations:

Evidence regarding consequences of use:

Copyright © 2000 by Merrill, an imprint of Prentice-Hall, Inc. All rights reserved.

TEST EVALUATION FORM CONTINUED

Reliability (cite manual page numbers) _____. Summarize data below.

Age or Grade	Type of reliability	Range of reliabilities (Total test)	Number Tested	Range of reliabilities (Part scores)

Standard errors of measurement _____   _____

Norms (cite manual page numbers) _____. Summarize data below.

    Type (e.g., percentile rank):

    Groups (size, age, or grade):

Separate norms (e.g., type of district):

Criterion-referenced interpretation

    Describe (if available):

Practical features

    Ease of administration:

    Ease of scoring:

    Ease of interpretation:

    Adequacy of manual and materials:

Comments of reviewers (See MMY or Test Critiques)

Summary Evaluation

    Advantages:

    Limitations:

(Why not have your instructor or a fellow student evaluate your items?)

Copyright © 2000 by Merrill, an imprint of Prentice-Hall, Inc. All rights reserved.

Exercise 18-C

EVALUATING AN ABILITY TEST

LEARNING GOAL: Evaluates a test using test evaluation form.

Directions: Select an aptitude test at the grade level of your choice and obtain a copy of the test, the manual, and other accessory material; your instructor can help you with this. Study the test materials, consult the reviews in the latest <u>Mental Measurements Yearbook</u> (MMY) and <u>Test Critiques</u>, and write your evaluation using the following test evaluation form. Be brief and include only the most essential information.

TEST EVALUATION FORM

Test title _____ Author(s)_____

Publisher _____ Copyright date(s) _____

Purpose of test _____

For grades (ages)_____ Forms _____

Scores available _____ Method of scoring _____

Administration time_____ Time(s) of parts _____

Validity (cite manual pages) _____. Summarize evidence below.

Content considerations:

Test-criterion relationships:

Construct considerations:

Evidence regarding consequences of use:

Copyright © 2000 by Merrill, an imprint of Prentice-Hall, Inc. All rights reserved.

TEST EVALUATION FORM CONTINUED

Reliability (cite manual page numbers) _____. Summarize data below.

Age or Grade	Type of reliability	Range of reliabilities (Total test)	Number Tested	Range of reliabilities (Part scores)

Standard errors of measurement _____   _____

Norms (cite manual page numbers) _____. Summarize data below.

    Type (e.g., percentile rank):

    Groups (size, age, or grade):

Separate norms (e.g., type of district):

Criterion-referenced interpretation

    Describe (if available):

Practical features

    Ease of administration:

    Ease of scoring:

    Ease of interpretation:

    Adequacy of manual and materials:

Comments of reviewers (See MMY or Test Critiques)

Summary Evaluation

    Advantages:

    Limitations:

(Why not have your instructor or a fellow student evaluate your items?)

Copyright © 2000 by Merrill, an imprint of Prentice-Hall, Inc. All rights reserved.

Exercise 18-D

ADMINISTERING PUBLISHED TESTS

LEARNING GOAL: Distinguishes between good and bad practices in administering published tests.

Directions: Indicate whether each of the following statements describes a **good (G)** practice or a **bad (B)** practice in administering a published test by circling the appropriate letter.

G   B   1.   Read the directions word for word.

G   B   2.   Give students extra time if there was an interruption during testing.

G   B   3.   If the directions didn't seem clear, tell the students again how to record their answers.

G   B   4.   Tell students what to do about guessing if the directions failed to include it.

G   B   5.   If asked about a particular item, tell the student: "I'm sorry but I cannot help you. Do the best you can."

G   B   6.   Make a record of any unusual student behavior during testing.

LEARNING GOAL: Describes a procedure for improving students' test-taking skills.

Directions: Briefly describe an ethical procedure a classroom teacher might follow for improving students' test-taking skills.

(Why not have your instructor or a fellow student evaluate your items?)

Turn up bottom of page for answers
Copyright © 2000 by Merrill, an imprint of Prentice-Hall, Inc. All rights reserved.

Answers to Selection 18-D

1. G 2. B 3. B
4. B 5. G 6. G

Exercise 18-E

USES OF PUBLISHED TESTS

LEARNING GOAL: Distinguishes between correct and incorrect statements concerning uses of published tests.

Directions: Indicate whether test specialists would **agree (A)** or **disagree (D)** with each of the following statements concerning **test use** by circling the appropriate letter.

A   D   1.   Published achievement tests are most useful in the areas of basic skills.

A   D   2.   Published achievement tests need **not** match the instructional objectives of the school.

A   D   3.   To detect underachievement, relatively large differences are needed between the scores of learning ability tests and achievement tests.

A   D   4.   Norm-referenced achievement tests are especially useful for individualizing instruction.

A   D   5.   Course grades are more valid when based on scores from published achievement tests.

A   D   6.   No important educational decision should be based on the scores of published tests alone.

LEARNING GOAL: Lists misuses of published tests.

Directions: List as many ways as you can think of that published test results might be misused. Use brief concise statements.

(Why not have your instructor or a fellow student evaluate your items?)

Turn up bottom of page for answers
Copyright © 2000 by Merrill, an imprint of Prentice-Hall, Inc. All rights reserved.

Answers to Selection 18-E

1. A   2. D   3. A
4. D   5. D   6. A

Exercise 19-A

USES OF CRITERION-REFERENCED AND NORM-REFERENCED INTERPRETATIONS

LEARNING GOAL: Relates test interpretation to the type of information needed.

Directions: For each of the following questions, indicate whether a **criterion-referenced (C)** or a **norm-referenced (N)** interpretation would be more useful by circling the appropriate letter.

C   N   1.   How does a student's test performance compare to that of other students in the same grade?

C   N   2.   What type of remedial work would be most helpful for a slow-learning student?

C   N   3.   How does a student's test performance in reading and mathematics compare.

C   N   4.   Which students' test performances exceed those of 90 percent of their classmates?

C   N   5.   Which students have achievement mastery of computational skills?

C   N   6.   How does student test performance in our school compare with that of other schools?

LEARNING GOAL: Describes the cautions needed when making criterion-referenced interpretations of tests designed for norm-referenced use.

Directions: List and briefly describe several factors to consider when using criterion-referenced interpretations with norm-referenced survey tests.

(Why not have your instructor or a fellow student evaluate your items?)

Copyright © 2000 by Merrill, an imprint of Prentice-Hall, Inc. All rights reserved.

Answers to Selection 19-A

1. N   2. C   3. N
4. N   5. C   6. N

Exercise 19-B

NATURE OF DERIVED SCORES

LEARNING GOAL: Distinguishes among the characteristics of different types of derived scores.

Directions: Indicate which type of derived score is described by each statement listed below by circling the appropriate letter. Use the following key.

KEY: G = grade equivalent scores, P = percentile rank, S = standard scores.

G   P   S   1.   Provides units that are based on the average score earned in different groups.

G   P   S   2.   Provides units that are **systematically unequal**.

G   P   S   3.   Provides units that are most nearly equal.

G   P   S   4.   Provides units that are most meaningful when interpreted with reference to normal curves.

G   P   S   5.   Provides units that are most meaningful at the elementary school level.

G   P   S   6.   Provides units that are easily interpreted and typically compare students with their own age group.

LEARNING GOAL: States the advantages and limitations of derived scores.

Directions: Briefly state one advantage and one limitation of percentile scores and standard scores.

Percentile Ranks
    Advantage:

    Disadvantage:

Standard Scores
    Advantage:

    Disadvantage:

(Why not have your instructor or a fellow student evaluate your items?)

Copyright © 2000 by Merrill, an imprint of Prentice-Hall, Inc. All rights reserved.

Answers to Selection 19-B

1. G 2. P 3. S
4. S 5. G 6. P

Exercise 19-C

GRADE EQUIVALENT SCORES

LEARNING GOAL: Distinguishes between appropriate and inappropriate interpretations of grade equivalent scores.

Directions: Indicate whether each of the following interpretations of grade equivalent (GE) scores are **appropriate (A)** or **inappropriate (I)** by circling the appropriate letter.

A   I   1.   A student who obtained a GE score of 3.1 in the spring of grade 4 would be expected to obtain a GE score of 4.1 in the spring of grade 5.

A   I   2.   A student in grade 4 who obtained a GE score of 4.7 in April scored higher than about half the students in the grade 4 norm group.

A   I   3.   A student with GE score of 5.3 in reading and 6.1 in math is performing better in math than in reading.

A   I   4.   A student who has GE scores in all subjects that are more than 1.5 above grade placement should probably be skipped to the next grade.

A   I   5.   A GE score of 11.0 for a grade 6 student indicates that the student did exceptionally well on the 6th grade content, but not that he or she could do grade 11 work.

A   I   6.   One year gains in GE scores for two students of 3.0 to 4.5 and 5.0 to 6.5 indicate equivalent amounts of progress.

LEARNING GOAL: State the advantages and limitations of grade equivalent scores.

Directions: Briefly state some of the major advantages and major limitations of grade equivalent scores.

Advantages:

Limitations:

(Why not have your instructor or a fellow student evaluate your items?)

Turn up bottom of page for answers
Copyright © 2000 by Merrill, an imprint of Prentice-Hall, Inc. All rights reserved.

Answers to Selection 19-C

1. I 2. A 3. I
4. I 5. A 6. I

Exercise 19-D

RELATIONSHIP OF DIFFERENT SCORING SYSTEMS

LEARNING GOAL: Converts scores from one scoring system to others.

Directions: Complete the following table by converting the given scores into comparable derived scores in the other scoring systems. Round your answers to the nearest whole number, except for z-scores where one decimal place should be reported. Assume that all score distributions are normal and based on a common reference group. The first row of scores, form a given z-score of 1.0 has been completed to illustrate the procedure. Try to complete the exercise without looking at the table in your book.

z-Score	T-Score	Standard Age Score (SD = 16)	Stanine	Percentile Rank
1.0	60	116	7	84
-1.0				
0.5				
-0.5				
	35			
	70			
		100		
		124		
0.7				
-1.3				

LEARNING GOAL: Explains the value of using score bands on test profiles.

Directions: Explain why it is desirable to plot scores on a test profile as **score bands** instead of specific **score points**.

(Why not have your instructor or a fellow student evaluate your items?)

Copyright © 2000 by Merrill, an imprint of Prentice-Hall, Inc. All rights reserved.

Exercise 19-E

___

INTERPRETATIONS OF SCORES ON PUBLISHED TESTS

LEARNING GOAL: Distinguishes between appropriate and inappropriate interpretations of scores on published tests.

Directions: Indicate whether test specialists would **agree (A)** or **disagree (D)** with each of the following statements about interpretations of scores on published tests by circling the appropriate letter.

A   D   1.   Percentile ranks of tests of the same subject can be used interchangeably.

A   D   2.   The percentile rank score does not require an assumption of a normal distribution.

A   D   3.   Information about a student's previous educational experiences and language background is used in interpreting test scores.

A   D   4.   A band that extends one standard error of measurement above and below a student's observed score helps guard against overly precise interpretations.

A   D   5.   Because the units on a grade equivalent scale are approximately equal, the difference between 4.0 and 5.0 can be treated as equivalent to that between 8.0 and 9.0.

A   D   6.   Before making an important decision based on a test score, the interpretation should be verified by other evidence.

LEARNING GOAL: States the advantages and limitations of using local norms.

Directions: Briefly state the advantages and limitations of using local norms to interpret test performance.

Advantages:

Limitations:

(Why not have your instructor or a fellow student evaluate your items?)

Copyright © 2000 by Merrill, an imprint of Prentice-Hall, Inc. All rights reserved.

Answers to Selection 19-E

1. D 2. A 3. A
4. A 5. D 6. A

Exercise A-1

MEASURES OF CENTRAL TENDENCY

LEARNING GOAL: Distinguishes among measures of central tendency.

Directions: For each of the following statements, indicate which **measure of central tendency** is being used by circling the appropriate letter using the following key.

KEY: A = Mean, B = Median, C = Mode.

A   C   1.   It is the most frequent score in a set of scores.

A   C   2.   It takes into account the numerical value of each score.

A   C   3.   It is **always** an actual score.

A   C   4.   It is **always** equal to the 50th percentile.

A   C   5.   It is determined by dividing the sum of a set of scores by the number of scores.

A   C   6.   It would **not** change if an extremely high score earned by a single individual was deleted from the set.

LEARNING GOAL: Selects the measure of central tendency that is most appropriate for a particular use.

Directions: For each of the following statements, indicate whether the mean (A) or the median (B) would be most appropriate by circling the letter.

A   B   1.   To use with the quartile deviation.

A   B   2.   To use with the standard deviation.

A   B   3.   To divide a set of scores into two equal halves.

A   B   4.   To compute a set of standard scores.

A   B   5.   To limit the influence of a single score of 85 when all the other scores range between 35 and 65.

A   B   6.   To report the most widely used measure of central tendency.

Turn up bottom of page for answers
Copyright © 2000 by Merrill, an imprint of Prentice-Hall, Inc. All rights reserved.

Answers to Selection A-1

(Top)   1. C   2. A   3. C   4. B   5. A   6. C
(Bottom) 1. B   2. A   3. B   4. A   5. B   6. A

Exercise A-2

MEASURES OF VARIABILITY

LEARNING GOAL: Distinguishes among the measures of variability.

Directions: For each of the following statements, indicate which **measure of variability** is being described by circling the appropriate letter using the following key.

KEY: A = Standard deviation, B = Quartile deviation, C = Range.

A   B   C   1.   It is based on the highest and lowest scores only.

A   B   C   2.   It is half the distance between the 25th and 75th percentiles.

A   B   C   3.   It is also called the semi-interquartile range.

A   B   C   4.   It takes into account the numerical value of each score.

A   B   C   5.   It is influenced least by adding one extremely low score.

A   B   C   6.   It can be used to identify the range of the middle 68 percent of scores in a normal distribution.

LEARNING GOAL: Selects the measure of variability that is appropriate for a particular use.

Directions: For each of the following statements, indicate which measure of variability would be most appropriate by circling the letter using the following key.

KEY: A = Standard deviation, B = Quartile deviation, C = Range.

A   B   C   1.   To obtain the most stable measure of variability.

A   B   C   2.   To obtain the simplest and quickest estimate of variability.

A   B   C   3.   To obtain the range of the middle 50 percent of a set of scores.

A   B   C   4.   To compute the amount of error in test scores.

A   B   C   5. To use with a small set of scores that includes one extremely high score.

A   B   C   6.   To compute a set T-scores.

Turn up bottom of page for answers
Copyright © 2000 by Merrill, an imprint of Prentice-Hall, Inc. All rights reserved.

Answers to Selection A-2

(Top)   1.C 2.B 3.B 4.A 5.B 6.A

(Bottom) 1.A 2.C 3.B 4.A 5.B 6.A

Exercise A-3

CONSTRUCTING GRAPHS AND COMPUTING MEASURES OF CENTRAL TENDENCY AND VARIABILITY

LEARNING GOAL: Constructs graphical representations of scores and computes measures of central tendency and variability.

Directions: Use the following set of scores to: (1) construct a frequency polygon with a class interval of three, (2) construct a stem and leaf diagram, and (3) compute the mean, median, range, and standard deviation.

Student	Score
A	60
B	58
C	56
D	54
E	53
F	52
G	48
H	47
I	45
J	42
K	40
L	39
M	37
N	35
O	32
P	29
Q	28
R	20
S	15
T	10

Median =
Range =
Mean =
Standard deviation =

Copyright © 2000 by Merrill, an imprint of Prentice-Hall, Inc. All rights reserved.

Answers to Selection A-3

```
STEM  LEAF
  6    0
  5    23468
  4    02578
  3    2579
  2    089
  1    05
```

Median = 41
Range = 50
Mean = 40
Standard deviation = 14

Exercise A-4

CORRELATION COEFFICIENT AND REGRESSION

LEARNING GOAL: Identifies the characteristics of the product-moment correlation coefficient.

Directions: Indicate whether each of the following features describes the product-moment correlation coefficient by circling **Yes** (if it does) and **No** (if it does not).

Yes   No   1.   During the computation, it takes into account the numerical value of each score.

Yes   No   2.   Is easy to compute without the aid of a calculator.

Yes   No   3.   Can be used to compute estimates of test reliability.

Yes   No   4.   Can be used to evaluated test-criterion relationships.

Yes   No   5.   The degree of relationship is shown by the **plus** and **minus** signs.

Yes   No   6.   Can be used to indicate the cause/effect relations between measurement variables.

LEARNING GOAL: Uses the regression equation to obtain predicted criterion scores from test scores.

Directions: The regression equation for predicting a criterion measure, Y, from a test score, X, is: predicted $Y = -1.0 + .4X$. Find the predicted criterion score for the following three students.

Carlos: Test score = 20

Predicted criterion score =

Kim: Test score = 15

Predicted criterion score =

Sam: Test score = 10

Predicted criterion score =

Turn up bottom of page for answers
Copyright © 2000 by Merrill, an imprint of Prentice-Hall, Inc. All rights reserved.

Answers to Selection A-4

1. Y 2. N 3. Y 4. Y 5. N 6. N
Predicted criterion scores: Carlos, 7; Kim, 5; Sam, 3

Exercise A-5

COMPUTING THE PRODUCT-MOMENT CORRELATION COEFFICIENT

LEARNING GOAL: Computes the product-moment correlation coefficient.

Directions: Compute the product-moment correlation for the pairs of scores in the following table.

Student	X	Y	X^2	Y^2	XY
A	15	16			
B	12	8			
D	13	11			
E	19	17			
F	10	9			
G	14	13			
H	11	5			
I	17	17			
J	11	9			

Turn up bottom of page for answers
Copyright © 2000 by Merrill, an imprint of Prentice-Hall, Inc. All rights reserved.

Answers to Selection A-5

Product-moment correlation = .86.